Cenozoic Fossils 1
Paleogene

Bruce L. Stinchcomb

Schiffer Publishing Ltd®

4880 Lower Valley Road, Atglen, Pennsylvania 19310

Dedication

This work, the fifth in a series on collectable fossils, represents a continuation of my book number four—The Cretaceous Period. As a first order item I dedicate this work to my parents, Leonard and Virginia Stinchcomb, who encouraged my strong interest in fossils and paleontology at an early age. With regards to the early Cenozoic and its fossils and strata—my first introduction to them, thanks to Len and Jean, involved the Florissant, Colorado, fossil beds, visited as an adolescent in the 1950s, which at that time was available for collecting fossils as part of a visit to the Colorado Petrified Forest. Other collecting trips with Len and Jean to Puryear, Tennessee, and Corinth, Tupelo, and Oxford, Mississippi, introduced me to additional early Cenozoic and late Cretaceous fossils—the former appearing in this work and many of the latter in my previously published book, *Mesozoic-II*, concerned with fossil of the Cretaceous Period.

Other Schiffer Books by Bruce L. Stinchcomb
Mesozoic Fossils: Triassic and Jurassic. ISBN: 9780764331633. $29.99
Mesozoic Fossils II: The Cretaceous Period. ISBN: 9780764332593. $29.99
Paleozoic Fossils. ISBN: 9780764329173. $29.95
World's Oldest Fossils. ISBN: 9780764326974. $29.95

Other Schiffer Books on Related Subjects
Whales and Seals: Biology and Ecology. Pierre-Henry Fontaine. ISBN: 9780764327919. $34.95

Copyright © 2010 by Bruce L. Stinchcomb
Library of Congress Control Number: 2009939149

Designed by Mark David Bowyer
Type set in Benguiat Bk BT / Aldine721 BT

ISBN: 978-0-7643-3424-5
Printed in China

Schiffer Books are available at special discounts for bulk purchases for sales promotions or premiums. Special editions, including personalized covers, corporate imprints, and excerpts can be created in large quantities for special needs. For more information contact the publisher:

Published by Schiffer Publishing Ltd.
4880 Lower Valley Road
Atglen, PA 19310
Phone: (610) 593-1777; Fax: (610) 593-2002
E-mail: Info@schifferbooks.com

For the largest selection of fine reference books on this and related subjects, please visit our web site at
www.schifferbooks.com
We are always looking for people to write books on new and related subjects. If you have an idea for a book please contact us at the above address.

This book may be purchased from the publisher.
Include $5.00 for shipping.
Please try your bookstore first.
You may write for a free catalog.

In Europe, Schiffer books are distributed by
Bushwood Books
6 Marksbury Ave.
Kew Gardens
Surrey TW9 4JF England
Phone: 44 (0) 20 8392-8585; Fax: 44 (0) 20 8392-9876
E-mail: info@bushwoodbooks.co.uk
Website: www.bushwoodbooks.co.uk
Free postage in the U.K., Europe; air mail at cost.

Contents

Acknowledgments

Various persons assisted and contributed to this work on fossils in a variety of ways, and they are specifically acknowledged in my previously published Schiffer books on fossils. In addition to these persons I wish to acknowledge the following; Brent Ashcraft of Benton, Mo., Christine Aide of Southwest Missouri State University, Carl Campbell of St. Louis Community College at Meramec, Richard Hagar of Arnold, Mo., Patricia Eicks of Mokane, Mo. For various assistance regarding Early Cenozoic geology and fossils of Germany, I wish to acknowledge the late A. Beirweiler of Echlishausen, Germany, Eugene and Lisa Hasher of Giengen/Brenz, the late Roland Kirsten and his wife Carin of Ulm, and R. Kuhn of Gunzburg, Germany. Last but not least, I would especially like to acknowledge John Stade of Ferguson, Mo., without whose focused work on Cenozoic fossils, especially those of Florida, this work would have less dimension.

Chapter One

The Cenozoic—
The Age of Mammals!

The Cenozoic Era, the youngest of the geologic eras, is sometimes known as "the age of mammals." This is the first of two books surveying this era with an emphasis on its collectable fossils. The Cenozoic Era is made up of seven subdivisions referred to as epochs—covered in this book are some fossils of the first three of these, the Paleocene, Eocene, and the Oligocene epochs.

The early Cenozoic (or Paleogene) represents a continuation of life of the late Mesozoic, but noticeably absent are those organisms which suffered extinction at the Cretaceous-Tertiary boundary (K/T boundary), one of the most abrupt and pronounced extinctions in the entire fossil record. The warm, subtropical climate of the late Mesozoic is continued through the Paleogene, but some of the notable fatalities of this **terminal Mesozoic extinction event** are the ammonites, belemnites, coiled oysters, rudistids, cycad-like plants, and, of course, the best known, the dinosaurs. Regarding vertebrates, it is not only dinosaurs that died off at this event, but also many of the other ruling reptiles like plesiosaurs, pterodactyls, and mosasaurs. Diversity of fossils, and the life they represent, after the K/T extinction is considerably reduced.

The earliest part of the Paleocene Epoch is especially limited in the diversity of its fossils (but not always in their abundance) compared to that diversity seen in the Cretaceous, before the K/T extinction event. By the Eocene Epoch diversity increases, especially so with mollusks, which besides microfossils, such as foraminifera, are usually the fossils of choice used in measuring diversity. This is a reasonable strategy as shelled mollusks (particularly gastropods), generally have left a more complete and extensive fossil record than has any other group in marine strata. Gastropod (as well as other invertebrates) **genera** thriving in the Eocene and Oligocene epochs are still with us today; however, specific species living in these epochs are generally extinct today. The end of the Oligocene is marked by another major extinction event—a phenomenon that has been observed independently by workers on marine invertebrates, mammals, and by paleobotanists. This extinction event ends the Paleogene!

With mammals, those of the early Cenozoic are generally somewhat archaic—some families are not yet represented and others, while represented, are primitive or bizarre. Also, a number of other mammal groups, such as the oreodonts, were common in the Paleogene, but then went extinct at the end of the Oligocene Ep-

och. Plants of the Paleogene, like those of today, were predominantly angiosperms, but they are generally represented by extinct species. Particularly noticeable with plants are the forms that are totally absent in the Paleogene—the grasses and other Monocots, as well as an absence of many herbaceous plant types.

Origin of the Subdivisions of the Cenozoic Era

The Cenozoic Era is that part of geologic time when life as we know it (especially higher life forms) developed—specifically it is that time when life forms like mammals, the social insects, and (many) flowering plants appeared and became widespread. In other words, the Cenozoic saw the appearance of the world we know today! It was during the Cenozoic, from sixty-seven million years ago until the present, that mammals became the top life forms.

The Cenozoic Era is divided into two, more or less equal parts: the Paleogene (or early Cenozoic) and the Neogene (or late Cenozoic). The Paleogene is made up of three subdivisions called epochs, the Paleocene, Eocene, and the Oligocene. Subdivisions delineating this last major portion of geologic time (and the strata representing such subdivisions) originally were proposed by Charles Lyell on the basis of percentages of marine mollusks found in its rocks. Lyell made the Eocene (early recent) that subdivision of the Cenozoic that had the lowest percentages of living species of marine mollusks—less than four percent (the Paleocene and Oligocene epochs were added later). The Miocene, the first (and earliest) epoch of the Neogene, had seventeen percent of its molluscan species still living and the Pliocene had around fifty percent living species. Today, additional epochs have been added—the Miocene, Pliocene, Pleistocene (ice age), and the Holocene constitute the Neogene, the youngest half of the Cenozoic Era.

Tertiary and Quaternary

The two periods of the Cenozoic, the Tertiary and the Quaternary, are vestiges of a late eighteenth century attempt at organizing the rock strata of the earth. The scheme originally included a primary and a secondary subdivision—primary rocks being those believed to have formed when the earth itself was formed—in other words they were thought to be "original" rocks of the Earth's crust. Primary rocks usually consisted of granite or other crystalline rock—rocks believed to have formed from the original **Creation**. Secondary rocks were hard, sedimentary rocks, which often, but not always, lacked fossils.

Tertiary rocks were sedimentary, like the secondary rocks, but they were softer still and less indurated (hardened), their fossils being more obvious and distinct—and more like life living today. Quaternary rock was soft—usually not rock at all but rather sand and clay often found along the banks of streams or near the tops of sea cliffs. Quaternary "rocks" were always found above all of the other types and were obviously young. The two original categories, primary and secondary, are no longer used. It has since been discovered that these apparently "young" rocks may be of many different ages and rocks like granite, although found at the "bottom of the stack," have never been found to represent any original crust of the earth—in fact, geologists are still looking to find such rock. Original crust may not exist anymore on the earth, but it does exist on the Moon and on other terrestrial planets like Mars—planets that have undergone **considerably less** geological activity than has the Earth. The term "Tertiary" still represents what it did before modern geology came about: those rocks whose fossils do not differ greatly from life forms of today. In modern terms, Tertiary refers to rock strata of the Paleocene, Eocene, Oligocene, Miocene, and Pliocene epochs, which are all younger than those rocks of the Mesozoic Era. Mesozoic Era rocks, by comparison, can contain some strange fossils like ammonites, belemnites, and dinosaurs, organisms essentially unrelated to anything living today.

Quaternary, like Tertiary, also refers (in a way) to the same thing it did when it was originally proposed. It's a useful term for identifying those superficial layers of sediment which are not cemented into real rock and which are found nearest the earth's surface, usually just below the soil. The Quaternary is made up of the Pleistocene Epoch (also known as the Ice Age) and the Holocene Epoch or recent time; it is also the shortest major subdivision of geologic time.

The Paleogene is framed at its bottom by the Mesozoic extinction event—that major extinction which ends the Mesozoic Era—and is topped by the end of the Oligocene, a time of major extinction of many mammals, mollusks, and some angiosperms. Paleogene fossils usually represent life forms somewhat close to those of today, but still different and more archaic, than are those of the Neogene.

Presented in the photos are a selection of Paleogene outcrops in North America.

Burnout in Paleocene Fort Union "Formation," southeastern Montana. Burnout is clay or shale fired from the spontaneous combustion of a coal seam. Burnout can sometimes contain nice leaf impressions.

Close-up of the
Paleocene burnout
portrayed in the
previous photo.

Petrified log (palm wood?) from the Paleocene Fort Union "Formation". Black Hills Petrified Forest, South Dakota.

Uranium prospect pit in Eocene Wind River Group sediments, Rattlesnake Range, central Wyoming. These non-marine strata were deposited by streams flowing from local uplifts in central Wyoming during the Eocene Epoch.

Large petrified tree from the Fort Union "Formation." Occasionally these petrified logs occur upright as this log is positioned; however, more commonly they lie prostrate on the ground where they have weathered from a clay or shale bed.

Soft, silty Eocene sandstone of the Wind River Group, Rattlesnake Range, Wyoming.

Brice Canyon, Utah. Tuffaceous siltstone of the Eocene Wasatch Group is shown here extensively eroded into these spires at Brice Canyon National Monument.

Spire of tuffaceous Eocene siltstone, Brice Canyon, Utah.

Interpretive sign describing Fossil Butte—the most productive region for Green River fossil fish is in this region. Since this picture was taken (1961), Fossil Butte has become Fossil Butte National Monument. Commercial fossil pits and quarries now operate in the formation to the west of here. The Fossil Butte deposits represent those sediments deposited in the Fossil Lake portion of the Green River Formation.

Looking north at Fossil Butte, 1961.

Outcrop of fossiliferous Green River Formation sediments of the Fossil Lake portion of the Green River Formation.

Side road to fossil fish bearing beds, 1961.

Green River slabby limestone of Lake Unita—Coalville, Utah.

Big Badlands National Monument, 1940: The upper portion of these beds is the Oligocene Brule Formation; the Chadron Formation composes the lower badlands to the left. The Chadron is now considered to be uppermost Eocene in age, rather than Oligocene. Note the unpaved entrance road at that time. *Courtesy of Warren Wagner.*

Outcrop of claystones of the Oligocene Brule Formation—Big Badlands National Monument, Scenic, South Dakota.

Badlands of the Brule Formation—South Dakota.

Close-up of Yellowstone Falls showing massive Eocene rhyolite that has been altered by hydrothermal activity since it was formed in the Eocene Epoch.

Yellowstone Falls, Yellowstone Park, northwest Wyoming. Yellowstone Falls is formed when the Yellowstone River en-counters and flows over a thick bed of Eocene rhyolite. Igneous activity in the Rocky Mountain region—associated with the mountain building begun in the late Mesozoic—was widespread during the early Cenozoic.

Late Oligocene volcanoclastic sediments intruded by horizontal layers of Miocene igneous rock (sills). Note the columns formed in the basalt-like igneous rock. This exposure is along the Yellowstone River in Yellowstone Park, northwestern Wyoming.

Tilted coal bearing strata exposed along the Alaskan Railway north of Mt. McKinley.
Tertiary strata in Alaska are almost always tectonically deformed and tilted in this manner.

Eocene Coal seam exposed along Alaskan Railway right-of-way.

Eocene volcanoclastic sediments exposed west of Yellowstone Park near Lakeview, Idaho. This strata was deposited considerably west of the current location of the hot spot, which, since the Eocene Epoch, has appeared to have moved eastward over 150 miles and is now directly under Yellowstone Park. What has actually happened is that the crust of North America has moved westward over the hot spot, which itself has remained stationary in the Earth's mantle.

18

Close-up of Paleogene volcanoclastic sediments of central Idaho that probably formed in part from Eocene volcanic activity over the Yellowstone hot spot.

Early Cenozoic (Eocene?) strata exposed in the San Francisco Bay area showing soft sediment deformation from presumed earthquakes on the San Andreas Fault. Note the boulders incorporated in the sandstone, presumable also carried to this location by early Cenozoic tectonic movement. Movement along the San Andreas Fault has been taking place since the mid-Mesozoic. This picture was taken in 1913.

Red clay makes up the badlands of the late Eocene Bridger Formation, located in southwestern Wyoming.

Collecting Cenozoic Fossils

Fossils of the Cenozoic Era represent some of the most collectable and attractive forms available. Many Cenozoic fossils are "eye candy" indeed! At times they can be large and spectacular. Because they represent that part of geologic time closest to the present, they can also be the most relevant fossils to many persons, being obviously related to life forms with which most persons are familiar. Fossil plants from Cenozoic rocks can be spectacular, even more so can be the mammals, as they are large in size and at times bizarre, yet still recognizable for what they are. Cenozoic mammals are indeed fascinating to many persons!

Cenozoic invertebrate fossils can be locally abundant and are often the fossils by which many persons get bitten by the "bug" of fossil collecting. Cenozoic limestone and marl can also yield their fossils with ease compared to older rocks, from which it is often more difficult to extricate fossils. Particularly collectable are many of the fossil plants from Cenozoic strata. Petrified wood, often looking like modern driftwood, is especially popular with rockhounds; leaf compressions and impressions are also collectable fossil plants. Rarer than either of these are fossil flowers and seeds.

Fossil fish and the rarer amphibians and reptiles are also quite desirable, but some of these may have considerable scientific value and a dictum among serious collectors is that scientific considerations take precedence over collecting. Articulated (complete) vertebrates in Cenozoic strata—especially those from strata that have not been extensively sampled, such as might turn up in an excavation—may well have significant scientific value.

Regarding articulated vertebrates, particularly noteworthy are the fossils of the Eocene Green River Formation of Wyoming, as well as similar age fossils from similar age lake sediments of Europe and China, the latter of which have come onto the fossil market during the last few years.

Strata of Cenozoic age appear to harbor more designated fossil sites than do most other parts of the geologic time scale. Designated (and usually well-known) Cenozoic fossil beds or sites in North America include the Florissant Fossil Beds (Florissant Fossil Beds National Monument), Fossil Butte of western Wyoming, the "John Day Fossil Beds" of Oregon, the "Big Bad Lands" of South Dakota, the Grey site of eastern Tennessee, and the La Brea Tar Pits of southern California. Europe also has its share of Cenozoic *Lagerstatten* designated as fossil sites, which include Grube Messel of Germany, the Oligocene Oeningen beds of Switzerland, and a number of sites in Italy like Monte Bolca, which is a Solnhofen-like, slabby limestone containing beautiful fossil fish. Cenozoic strata can be sources for large, spectacular fossils, some of which are specifically quarried for fossils, which become part of the "Geo-decor Industry." These include the spectacular fish, stingrays, and palms of the Eocene Green River Formation of Wyoming.

Cenozoic strata can be a prolific source of fossil fuels such as coal, lignite, and oil shale. Some of these occurrences, like that of Grube Messel in Germany, as a consequence of past mining activity, have yielded significant fossil specimens as a by-product of such activity. Shale and clay beds, as well as the lignite itself, of the Fort Union Formation in the US, have the potential for yielding, if not specimens new to science, at least specimens which should go toward education—the fossil leaves illustrated here are a case in point. Generally, however, in large mining operations like those of the Fort Union Formation, collecting (more specifically what is really the salvage of fossils) is discouraged and is rarely done. This should not be the case. Efforts should be made to recover a reasonable amount of the fossils unearthed as a consequence of mining for use in paleontology and education.

The Green River Formation is another example of a potential fossil bonanza if the oil shales of the formation were to be mined for petroleum—an issue that keeps popping up but which currently does not appear to be practical. On this matter, attitudes taken by some governmental agencies toward collectors practicing avocational paleontology by working former oil shale test pits appears unfavorable, as do some positions taken by the Society for Vertebrate Paleontology (SVP and SAFE). Allowing fossil material to be collected, instead of being buried or destroyed, encourages various levels of scientific activity amongst a variety of interested amateur groups, provides a "hands on" experience that increases and encourages interest in fossils, and makes materials available for educational use.

Restrictions and prohibitions on collecting Cenozoic fossils have often been triggered by the frequent occurrence of vertebrates in rocks of this age. Vertebrate fossils particularly seem to elicit a protectionist mind-set by persons who otherwise would have little or no understanding of or interest in fossils or geology. Many Cenozoic fossil localities worldwide appear to have been made less accessible to avocational paleontology as a consequence of their containing vertebrate fossils, many of which are common forms and of little or no interest to science. Institutions and governmental agencies dealing with this issue should at least be neutral and not focused upon discouraging an activity through which citizens acquire an interest in, and understanding of, science. The attitude that it is better for specimens to be destroyed or left in the ground than to benefit interested persons is not only a mean-spirited one but, to the author at least, is also counterproductive to the broad interests of science and paleontology.

The author's well organized (and labeled) fossil collection—1955, which includes some of the fossils illustrated here.

Period	Epoch	Age	Age my.
		Present	0
Quaternary	Neogene	Holocene	
		Pleistocene	
		Pliocene	
Tertiary		Miocene	
	Paleogene	Oligocene	
		Eocene	
		Paleocene	67 K/T extinctions
	Upper Cretaceous	Maastrichtian	
		Campanian	
		Santonian	
		Coniacian	

Geologic time scale of the Cenozoic Era.

Value range used in this book

The following value range index is used for specimens illustrated in this book:

A $1,000-$1,500
B $500-$1,000
C $250-$500
D $100-$250
E $50-$100
F $25-$50
G $10-$25
H $1.00-$10.00

Bibliography

Case, Girard. *A Pictorial Guide to Fossils.* New York: Van Nostrand Reinhold Company, 1982.

Fenton, C. L. and M. A. Fenton. *The Fossil Book.* Doubleday and Company, 1958.

Gould, Stephen J. "Sea, Drugs, Disasters, and the Extinction of Dinosaurs" *in The Flamingo's Smile-Reflections in Natural History.* New York, London: W. W. Norton Co., 1985.

"Lyell's Pillars of Wisdom" *in The Lying Stones of Marrakech, Penultimate Reflections in Natural History.* New York: Three Rivers Press, 2000.

Chapter Two
Plants, Fungi, and "Monerans"

Nitrogen Fixing Bacteria

Legumous angiosperms may have first appeared in the late Mesozoic or the early Cenozoic.

Could these be the rootlets of a legume? Rootlets preserved in quartz of a possible leguminous angiosperm. Sometime in the Mesozoic Era symbiosis between angiosperms and nitrogen fixing bacteria developed, enabling such a plant to "fix" nitrogen from the atmosphere and form nitrogen compounds by the addition of small nodules harboring a bacterium. This was a significant symbiotic evolutionary development, which occurred between plants and monerans. Fort Union Formation, Paleocene Epoch, North Dakota. Found as a pebble in Missouri River gravels.

Monerans (Stromatolites)

Stromatolites are structures produced by the physiological activities of primitive, photosynthetic life forms, usually photosynthetic monerans (previously known as blue-green algae). Fossil stromatolites represent the oldest, direct evidence of life on the earth, having been found in rocks as old as 3.5 billion years. They are still forming today, the monerans that form them can be found living and forming these stony structures in very localized areas. Geologically young stromatolites are able to form only in an environment where higher life forms are absent. The presence of animal life will result in browsing or cropping of the stromatolites, thus destroy them. Paleogene stromatolites shown here formed in large lakes that covered major parts of the western United States. These sediments, deposited during the Eocene Epoch, make up the well-known Green River Formation. Sediments of the Green River Formation were deposited in fresh, brackish, and hypersaline lakes that covered large parts of western Colorado, Utah, and Wyoming. Reef-like stromatolites formed locally in these lakes when the water was hypersaline, especially in parts of Wyoming where the stromatolite masses are now relished by rockhounds who cut and polish them into agate jewelry or bookends, the stromatolites being referred to as "algae agate."

Chlorellopsis coloniata sp. This is a stromatolite, a structure produced by the physiological activity of cyanobacteria. Stromatolites can be common fossils locally in the Eocene Green River Formation of central Wyoming, where they formed in large, shallow lakes. Fossil stromatolites are the earliest direct evidence of life on the earth, some of them going back to as far as 3.5 billion years to the early Precambrian. (Value range F).

Chlorellopsis coloniata sp. Part of a stromatolite colony from the Upper Eocene Green River Formation, stromatolites locally can be common and interesting fossils. They were (and are) produced by the physiological activities of moneras—the cyanobacteria that produce them are also known as blue green algae. This is from part of a large colony of Eocene, Green River stromatolites, which occur near Wamsutter, Wyoming.

Gymnosolen sp. This is a stromatolite with small "fingers" from the Green River Formation, Upper Eocene. Wamsutter Wyoming. (Value range F).

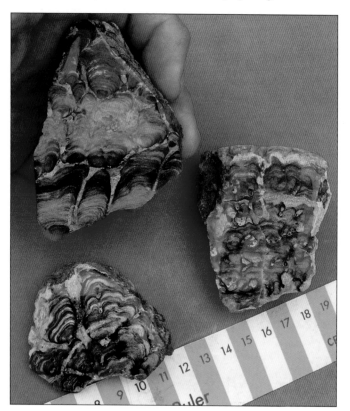

Collenia. sp. Specimens of this long ranging and attractive stromatolite form genus come from the Eocene Green River Formation, Lake Gosuite deposits. A number of such nicely polished stromatolites are currently on the fossil market and have been widely distributed by collectors. Wamsutter, Wyoming. (Value range G).

Gymnosolen sp. Presented here is the same specimen as in the previous photo. Stromatolites are given names known as form genera, allowing the many variations found in the fossil record to be distinguished. The genus *Gymnosolen* is such a form genus.

Gymnosolen sp. This is another specimen of this stromatolite form genus, looking down at the top of a group of stromatolite "fingers".

Fungi

The fungi are an ancient group that have left a scant and puzzling fossil record.

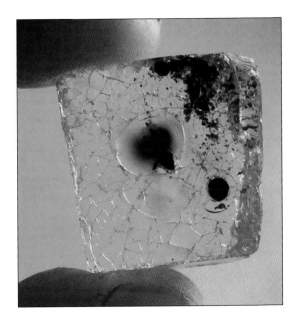

Mold (on an insect) in a fossil resin: Representatives of the kingdom fungi are uncommon fossils, although the degradational effects of them on dead animal and plant tissue can be seen in the fossil record at least since the Paleozoic. Most fungi are very fragile and would normally not be preserved, except in some exotic medium such as this fossil resin. (Value range F).

Division Bryophyta: These are believed to be fossil mosses. Bryophytes (which includes the mosses) are primitive non-vascular plants, which grow in wet or damp places. Their fossil record is meager but it is better in the Cenozoic than in earlier parts of geologic time. This presents a paleontological puzzle. It is still unclear how diverse and widespread bryophytes were in the deep time of the late Precambrian and the Paleozoic. They have left little fossil record in either, but should have been abundant, or at least locally present; however, their presence deep into the Precambrian is doubtful.

Hypnites arkansana Whittlake, Mosses. These fossil mosses were associated with large petrified logs found in the Wilcox Formation near Jonesboro, Arkansas; one of the large logs is illustrated in chapter 1.(Value range G).

Hypnites arkansana Whittlake. Moss. The Bryophytes have left a meager fossil record. They represent part of a large group of non-vascular plants existing since at least the Devonian Period of the Paleozoic Era. Their existence in the Earth's early biosphere may go back considerably before that, although their earlier fossil record is quite muddy and sparse. These fossils have been described as representing fossil mosses, however, they could equally be the leaves of a conifer known as *Glyptostrobus*, which in some specimens resemble a moss. Wilcox Group, Jonesboro, Arkansas. (Value range F).

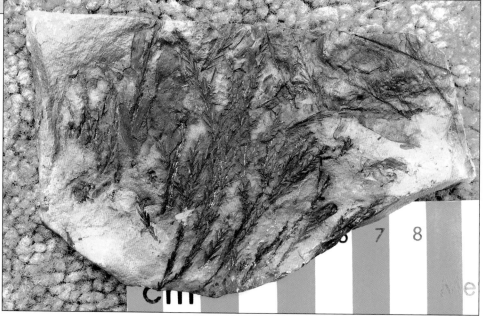

Mosses or conifer twigs. Fossils quite similar to those found in the Wilcox Formation of Arkansas are found in the Paleocene Fort Union Formation of North Dakota. Often it is difficult to distinguish between a fossil moss and a conifer of the genus *Glyptostrobus*, which can resemble a fossil moss (Value range F).

Pteridophytes (ferns): Ferns have been widespread and successful plants, which have left a good fossil record since the late Paleozoic.

Fern. *Dennstaedlia blomstrandii.* This is a fern found in Paleocene strata just above the K-T boundary and found below it as well in similar rocks of the late Cretaceous (Hell Creek Formation). Paskapoo Formation, Alberta, Canada. (Value range F).

Climbing fern from the Green River Formation, Douglas Pass, Garfield County, Colorado.

Lygodium kaulfussii (climbing fern). These ferns occur in lake deposits of the Wasatch Formation, which becomes the Green River Formation farther to the west. Moneta, Natrona County, Wyoming.

Salvinia sp. A water fern. Water ferns (also known as duckweed fern) are small, specialized ferns that live in still, warm waters and float on the water surface like duckweed. Today, they are native to warm waters of South America, but in the Paleogene *Salvinia* had a wide range, often occurring at high latitudes. A smaller water fern of the genus *Azolla* has been found to have been present in vast numbers in the Arctic Ocean during the Eocene, where carbonaceous layers composed of it are found in deep sea sediments of the Arctic Ocean. These specimens of *Salvinia* occur as impressions in burnout of the Fort Union "Formation" near Ranchester, Wyoming.

Arthrophytes: Arthrophytes of the Cenozoic Era were similar to those living today. In the Paleozoic, and to some degree in the early Mesozoic, arthrophytes were often represented by large plants such as calamites. In the Cenozoic, they were more modest in size, like the modern forms shown here.

Equsitum fluviatile. A group of living, small species of this arthrophyte—a good example of a modern "living fossil."

Equsitum sp. A scouring rush (Division Arthrophyta) from the Upper Eocene, Green River Formation, Douglas Pass, Garfield County, Colorado. (Value range F).

Equsitum sp. Another living example of what was, in the geologic past, a much more widespread plant—abundant particularly during the late Paleozoic as the arthrophyte genus *Calamites*.

Gymnosperms

Cone bearing plants (gymnosperms) were common in the early Cenozoic, their biomass during the Paleocene and Eocene sometimes making up thick beds of coal or lignite. Lignite beds are particularly widespread in the Paleocene Fort Union "*Formation" of Montana, Wyoming, the Dakotas, and in the equivalent Paskapoo Formation of Alberta and Saskatchewan. These lignite beds are extensively mined near Gillette, Wyoming, Coalstrip, Montana, and central North Dakota, where they are thick and low in sulfur. This Cenozoic coal (or lignite) originated primarily from gymnosperms, particularly metasequoia and sequoia. Sometimes this lignite is full of small "blebs" of amber-like fossil resin, which is generally highly fractured. This fossil resin, derived from these ancient conifers, is the source of cresylic acid, a feedstock used in making plastic (the plastic currently used in making soft drink bottles). Huge amounts of this gymnosperm-derived lignite is retorted (heated), producing gaseous fuels (synfuels) and cresylic acid as well as other useful chemical and chemical by-products, including the rare noble gas xenon.

*The Fort Union Formation has been promoted to being a group of formations, of which the Golden Valley Formation of North Dakota produces Ginko leaves in ironstone. Older literature will have the Fort Union as a formation; more recent literature will have it as a group.

Taxodium sp. (bald cypress). Large forests of this primitive conifer existed over the middle portion of North America during the Paleocene—the earliest part of the Cenozoic. Forests of these water-loving trees existed for thousands of years at one place forming beds of coal, which now is mined extensively in North Dakota, South Dakota, and in parts of Wyoming. Specimen from the Fort Union Group, Golden Valley Formation, Mandan, North Dakota.

Taxodium sp. (bald cypress) with cone compression. Paskapoo Formation, Paleocene, Alberta.

Metasequoia occidentalis (Newberry). This is a primitive conifer whose vegetation is similar to, and often difficult to distinguish from, that of *Taxodium* (the bald cypress). These leaves come from strata just above the Cretaceous-Tertiary boundary (Fort Union "Formation," Jordan, Montana. (Value range F).

Sequoia sp. Leaves of this mature conifer are preserved in ironstone. *Sequoia* and *Metasequoia* leaves, which formed at an early stage of growth, differ considerable from mature ones that have been on the plant for some time. Golden Valley Formation, Fort Union Group ("Formation"), Mandan, North Dakota. (Value range F).

Close up of a coal chunk containing fractured resin blobs (amber?). Little Tonzona River, Alaska.

Metasequoia occidentalis (Newberry). Fort Union "Formation," North Dakota.

Shown here is an outcrop of burnout in the Fort Union Group, southeastern Montana. Clay or shale beds in the Fort Union (the Paskapoo Formation of Canada) can contain thick coal or lignite beds. At some time in the geologic past, this coal caught fire through spontaneous combustion. The burning coal fired the clay layers to a brick red color. In some layers of burnout, leaf impressions can be found. Beds of burnout sometimes are dug out for road material, which, when crushed, makes reddish colored roads that are often seen while driving through the northern high plains.

Taxodium sp. (bald cypress). Impressions of the leaves of this primitive conifer are preserved in burnout. This brick red rock is baked or fired shale from beds overlying a coal seam that has combusted naturally, often tens, hundreds, or thousands of years ago. These red layers contrast with the somber colored shale (Somber beds) and carbonaceous clays, which characterize much of the Fort Union "Formation." Southeastern Montana. (Value range F).

Metasequoia sp. + angiosperm (*Betula* sp., beech). Fort Union "Formation," Jordan, Montana.

Taxodium sp. This is the same specimen as in the previous photo with different lighting. Fossil leaves in burnout are best observed in a shadow, where they then can show up distinctively. Unlike compression fossils, where some of the carbon of the leaf still exists, with burnout no original plant material occurs.

Metasequoia sp. (right) and *Sequoia* sp. (left). From the Paleocene equivalent of the Fort Union "Formation" in Alberta, the Paskapoo Formation. These plant bearing beds of the Paleocene occurring north of the US-Canadian border reveal the same flora as found in the states.

Metasequoia occidentalis Eocene, White Lake, British Columbia, Canada. (Value range F).

Metasequoia sp. Beds of early Cenozoic strata (often with coal beds) occur along the western part of North America from Oregon north to Alaska. These redwood leaves come from near Palmer, Alaska, north of Anchorage.

Metasequoia (left) and *Taxodium* (right) from Eocene strata, Kamloops Group, Tranquille tuffaceous shale, Cache Creek, British Columbia, Canada.

Taxodium sp. Tranquille Shale, Kamloops Group, Eocene, Cache Creek, British Columbia, Canada.

Glyptostrobus sp. A primitive conifer often associated with metasequoia. Some impressions of *Glyptostrobus* can be difficult to distinguish from fossil mosses. Eocene, Gardner, Montana. (Value range F).

Glyptostrobus sp. (with cone). Paskapoo Formation, Paleocene, Alberta. (Value range E).

These fern-like conifers represent mature leaves of *Glyptostrobus*. *Glyptostrobus* is a diagnostic, early Cenozoic conifer. Fort Union Formation, Jordan, Montana.

Taxodium sp., Eocene, Lakeview, Idaho.

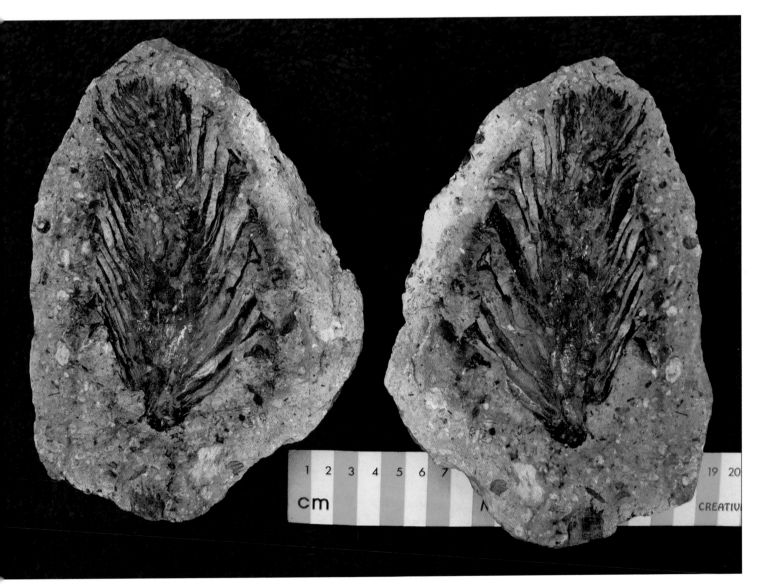

Conifer cone preserved in a large concretion. Oligocene, Italy. (Value range E).

Fort Union Petrified Wood

A large quantity of petrified and lignitized wood occurs in the Fort Union Group and its correlatives. Much of this wood appears to be from conifers but that of angiosperms occurs with equal abundance. The co-nifers *sequoia*, *metasequoia*, and *taxodium* are abundantly represented in the Fort Union Group by their leaves. As the identification of fossil wood requires the making of thin sections and work with a microscope, these two wood types (conifer vs. gymnosperm) are not identified in this work.

Fort Union Formation badlands—San Juan Basin, New Mexico. Badlands like these in the Fort Union "Formation" can contain large quantities of petrified wood of various types eroding from its gullies.

Badlands and petrified wood, San Juan Basin, New Mexico. Badlands like these in the Fort Union "Formation" can contain large amounts of petrified wood of various types.

Petrified log, South Dakota. Logs of petrified wood can be common in some beds of the Fort Union "Formation."

Petrified log—palm wood? South Dakota, Fort Union "Formation."

Ginkos

Ginkos represent a division of seed bearing trees paleobotanists consider to have evolved independently of the angiosperms. Ginkos survived the Cretaceous extinction event and can locally be abundant fossils in rocks of early Cenozoic age. The ginkos shown here came from the Fort Union Group, Golden Valley Formation in North Dakota, and the equivalent Paskapoo Formation of Saskatchewan. Not too far above the K/T boundary, the Fort Union Group, Golden Valley Formation has produced a large number of fossil ginko leaves preserved in layers of ironstone—leaves that have been widely distributed by collectors. Ginkos were known as fossils before the living trees were discovered growing on the grounds of a Buddhist Monastery in southeastern Asia. Apparently they survived as a consequence of the activities of man rather than the usual opposite scenario culminating in extinction. Cenozoic ginko leaves like these North Dakota specimens are similar to those living today.

Group of *Ginko adiantoides* leaves. Golden Valley Formation of Fort Union Group, Almont, North Dakota.

Ginko adiantoides—group of leaves. Golden Valley Formation, Fort Union Group, Almont, North Dakota. (Value range F, single leaf).

Single *Ginko adiantoides.*
Although these fossil leaves are
distinguished from the modern
Ginko biloba, they appear to be
morphologically identical. (Value
range F).

Ginko adiantoides. Paskapoo Formation, Alberta.

Ginko adiantoides. Paskapoo Formation, southern Alberta.

Angiosperms

These are the dominant plants of the Cenozoic Era and they are the dominant plants over large portions of the earth today. Seeds and flowers are the hallmark of an angiosperm, as well as the leaves shown here from the Fort Union and Paskapoo Formations. Beds of shale, clay, sandstone, and coal (lignite) make up these formations, which locally can contain numerous fossil plants. The fossil plants are usually leaf compressions or impressions, as well as petrified or lignitized wood. The Fort Union flora is predominantly a subtropical one consisting of conifers and angiosperms. The equivalent Paskapoo Formation in Canada (geological nomenclature sometimes changes at political boundaries) covers sizeable parts of the prairie provinces of Alberta and Saskatchewan. The flora of these formations has been documented in a number of works by the U S and Canadian geological surveys.

Cyclocarya sp. Flower in ironstone. An example of an early fossil flower—a reproductive structure distinctive of the angiosperms. Golden Valley Formation, Fort Union Group, Mandan, North Dakota. (Value range F).

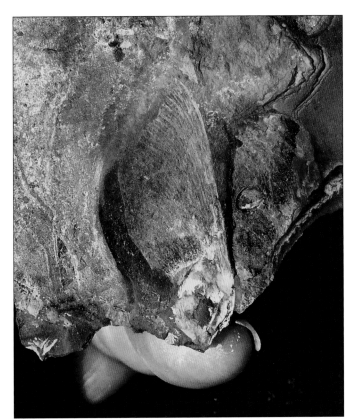

Acer sp. Maple seed preserved in ironstone, Mandan, North Dakota. (Value range F).

Platanus raynoldsi Newberry. Fort Union "Formation," North Dakota.

Group of typical Fort Union angiosperm leaves. North Dakota.

Poplar. Fort Union Group, Cody Wyoming. (Value range F).

Betula (Beech). Lake Sakagewea, North Dakota. (Value range F).

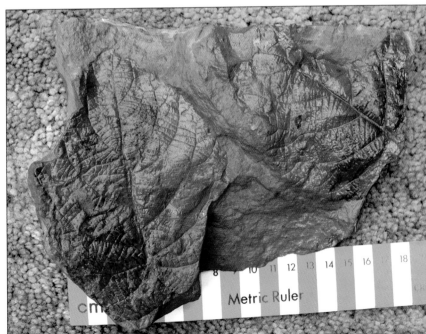

Eucommia serrata + metasequoia. Paskapoo Formation, Alberta.

Cornus sp. (Dogwood).
Paskapoo Formation,
Paleocene southern Al-
berta. (Value range F).

Sapindus affrinis Newberry. These leaf impressions are preserved in burnout from the Fort Union Group, Ranchester, Wyoming.

Ampelopsis. Fort Union Group, Paleocene, Cody, Wyoming.

Viburnum asperum. Fort Union
Group, Glendive, Montana.

Platanus (Sycamore). A
very large leaf, Fort Union
Group, North Dakota.

Acer sp. (Maple). Fort Union
Group, Cody, Wyoming. (Value
range F).

Plants of the Wilcox Group

One of the most extensive and diverse floras of early Cenozoic plants occurs in clay lenses of what is known as the Wilcox Group of the southeastern United States. The Wilcox flora is one of Eocene tropical plants, a flora predominantly of angiosperms. Most Wilcox plants are preserved as compressions (compressed leaves with some original material preserved) in clay or claystone. Clays yielding these Wilcox leaves generally occur in lens-shaped beds deposited in fresh or brackish water lagoons. Plants of the Wilcox are diverse in their variety, with more species and genera known than are found in similar age floras of the western U S. The Eocene Wilcox flora most closely resembles that found living today in the Caribbean.

Most Wilcox plants illustrated here have come from Tennessee, Mississippi, and Arkansas. Considering the extensive area covered by the Wilcox Group, its flora could be enlarged with additional serious collecting. One of the areas of Wilcox outcrop is Crowley's Ridge in northeastern Arkansas and southeast Missouri. This region, one that has a potential for additional fossil plants, has been seriously worked in the early and mid-twentieth century by only two people—both associated with what at the time were state teacher colleges. Missouri Wilcox plants were collected and studied by Albert S. Duckworth of what was Southeastern Missouri State Teachers College (now Southeast Missouri State University) and those of northeastern Arkansas by Eugene B. Wittlake of Arkansas State University, Jonesboro, Arkansas.

Outcrop of leaf bearing sandstone layers of the Lower Eocene Wilcox Group near Jonesboro, Arkansas, Crowley's Ridge. The Wilcox Group yields an extensive flora of tropical plants (primarily angiosperms) similar in some ways to modern trees of the Caribbean.

Clay beds of the Wilcox Group were sometimes deposited in ponds or lagoons similar to this. Waters of the Wilcox lagoons were particularly calm, allowing fine clay to cover sinking leaves and gently bury them. Water lilies like these are believed to have covered these lagoons, further protecting the clay at the bottom from disturbance.

Rocky hillside of leaf bearing sandstone of the Eocene Wilcox Group near Paragould, Arkansas.

Group of Wilcox plants, Puryear, Tennessee. Tropical floras characterize the early Cenozoic. This is a group of angiosperm leaves from the Lower Eocene, Wilcox Group of Tennessee. The leaves are found in layers of clay and represent one of the largest and most diverse Eocene floras known. Besides these fossil leaves from Tennessee, most of the other Wilcox leaves shown here are from Crowley's Ridge in eastern Arkansas. The Wilcox has a large angiosperm flora related to that currently found in the West Indies. Its flora has been documented in a number of publications, mostly those (Professional Papers) of the U.S. Geological Survey.

Another group of Wilcox plants. Note that the majority of Wilcox leaves have smooth edges (entire margined). Smooth edged angiosperms are more characteristic of warm climates. Angiosperm leaves from more temperate climates tend to be toothed or lobed. (Value range F or G, single specimen).

Clay pit at Puryear, Tennessee, 1955. Loess comprises the upper thick sequence of beds of the Pleistocene age. The lower layers are clays of the Holly Springs Member of the Wilcox Group—the leaf bearing layers being the lower beds of the clay lens. These leaf bearing clay lenses were exposed in clay mining activities.

Collecting leaves at Puryear, Tennessee: the author in on the left, on the right is Virginia Stinchcomb, 1955.

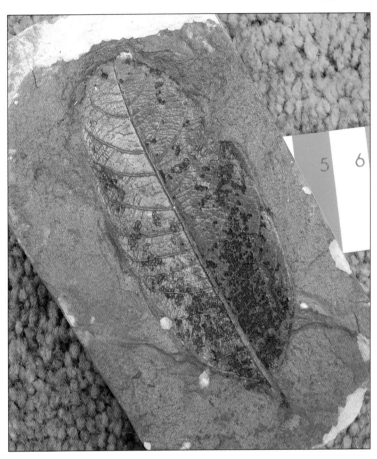

Author with leaf slab, 1955, Puryear, Tennessee.

Capparis eocenica Berry. Tropical leaf type. Wilcox Group, Puryear, Tennessee.

Diospyros wilcoxiana Berry. Wilcox Group, Ackerman clay, Holly Springs Member, Puryear, Tennessee.

Magnolia (fired). Wilcox Group, Puryear, Tennessee.

Magnolia sp. Wilcox Group, Holly Springs Member, Puryear, Tennessee. (Value range F).

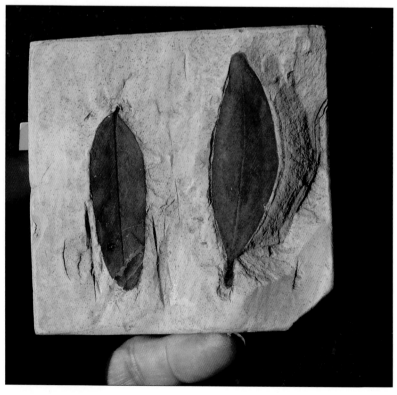

Sophora mucronata Berry. Pair of leaves. Wilcox Group, Holly Springs sand, Puryear, Tennessee.

Tropical Fruit, Puryear, Tennessee.

Fig leaf with insect nibble preserved in sandstone. "Hardy's Mill," Jonesboro, Arkansas. The Hardy's Mill locality was located from old (1850s pre-Civil War) literature and found to yield nice fossils from the Wilcox Group. Old literature can be a good source of forgotten fossil localities. (Value range F).

Cassia sp. Leaf with veins of leaf showing distinctly.

Large petrified log. Jonesboro, Arkansas. This log was found and moved by a farmer using a tractor where it was positioned next to a barn in 1957. The following Wilcox leaves preserved in blue-gray claystone came from beds associated with this log.

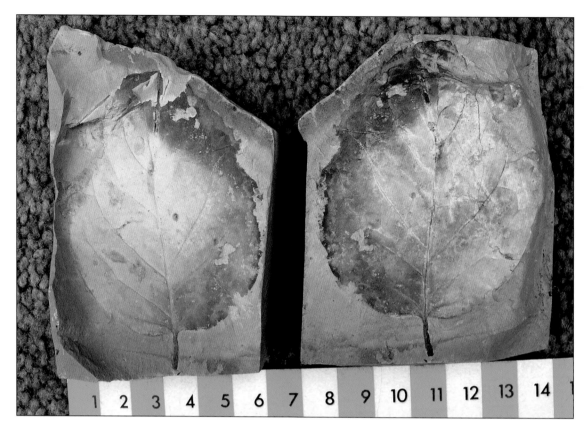

Ficus sp. (Fig). Hardy's Mill Locality, Jonesboro, Arkansas. (Value range F).

Betula sp. (Beech). Iron stained leaf, Jonesboro, Crowley's Ridge, Arkansas. (Value range F).

Close-up of previous leaf on the right.

This leaf has been extensively eaten by insects. A specimen like this shows extensive insect-plant interaction even though insects are rare fossils in the leaf bearing beds of the Wilcox Group. Jonesboro, Arkansas, Crowley's Ridge. (Value range F).

Betula sp. Heavily iron oxide stained leaf. Crowley's Ridge, Arkansas.

Leaf bearing clay outcrop, Oxford, Mississippi, 1955.

Lightly iron oxide stained leaf. Crowley's Ridge, Arkansas.

Oreopanyx sp. Hematite stained leaf on white clay. These leaf fossils are stunning with their preservation as iron oxide stains on kaolin. Oxford, Mississippi. (Value range E).

Cinnamon sp. Leaf preserved by red hematite stain on white clay. Wilcox Group, Oxford, Mississippi. (Value range F).

Ficus sp. (Fig). Wilcox Group, Oxford, Mississippi. (Value range E, pair).

Plants of the Late Eocene Jackson Group

The late Eocene Jackson Group of the Gulf coastal plain yields a tropical flora similar to (but not as diverse as) that of the Wilcox Group. The plants found generally are angiosperms and petrified wood.

Scattering of leaves and leaf fragments in kaolin. Clay lenses formed locally in lagoons can sometimes contain numerous leaf compressions like these. Groups of fragmented leaves like these are generally less desirable then are single, complete leaves. Claiborne Group, Upper Eocene, north of Houston, Texas. (Value range G for similar material).

Group of leaves, Jackson Group, Red Bluff, Arkansas. These leaves date to the late Eocene in age. The Jackson Group has a tropical flora somewhat similar to that of the Wilcox Group.

Group of tropical angiosperm leaves. Jackson Group. North of Houston, Texas.

Palms

Fossil palm leaves and wood are particularly desirable plant fossils. The early Cenozoic was characterized by a tropical climate over a large portion of the globe, which apparently was one of the warmest periods of geologic time. Fossils of palms locally can occur with some abundance in Eocene strata. These palm impressions and palm wood samples come from the southern US; however, similar fossil palms are found in Eocene strata of Wyoming, Montana, and Canada.

Petrified log of palm wood, Northern Mississippi. Petrified palm wood has a distinctive "dotted" pattern when sliced. This fossil wood comes from beds of the Wilcox Group in Mississippi, Arkansas, and Louisiana, as well as from southeastern Texas. Polished rounds of petrified palm wood are popular with rock hounds and have been widely distributed. Wilcox Group, Lower Eocene. (Value range F, polished round).

Sabalites grayanus (Lesquereux). This is a palm leaf from a sandstone bed of the Wilcox Group, Hardy's Mill, Jonesboro, Arkansas. This is a nice palm leaf impression in sandstone of the Wilcox Group. (Value range D).

Slabs (rounds) of palm wood, Wilcox Group, northern Louisiana. Sometimes rounds like this are made into faces of a clock by the addition of a clock movement. Palms were a dominant plant in the Eocene, sometimes occurring at relatively high latitudes in what has been considered to have been one of the warmest periods of the Earth's recent geologic history—forty-five million years in terms of geologic time being relatively recent. (Value range F, single polished round).

Narrow sabal palm. Red Bluff, Arkansas. (Value range E).

Sabalites sp. Palm, part and counterpart. Jackson Group, Upper Eocene. Red Bluff on Arkansas River near Pine Bluff, Arkansas. (Value range D).

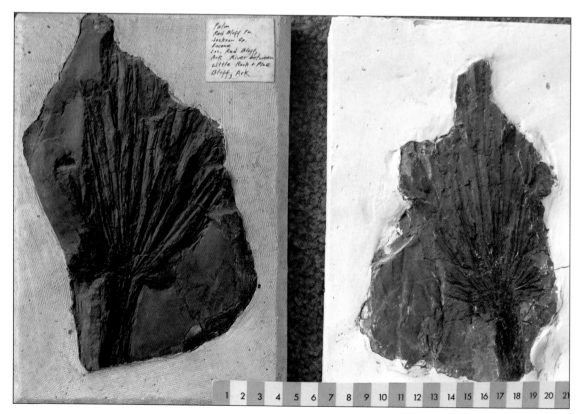

Here is a closer look at the single specimen seen in the previous photo.

Plants of the Green River Formation

The Upper Eocene Green River Formation is most famous for its fossil fish. However, fossil leaves, including whole branches bearing their leaves and giant palms, are found also, the latter being found where the formation is quarried for its fossil fish. These large fossil plants are spectacular and, understandably, they can be quite pricey where they are used in what is known as "geo-decor." Here is a group of more modest Green River leaves from the extensive shallow lake deposits of the Green River Formation of Utah and western Colorado (Lake Unita).

Gilsonite vein in the Green River Formation, Bonanza, Utah, 1964. These are outcrops in the Lake Unita portion of the Green River Formation.

Outcrop of the Green River Formation. Green River, Wyoming.

Platanus (Macqinitiea) wyomingensis (California sycamore), Green River Formation, Bonanza, Utah. These leaves are often referred to as sweet gum leaves. Although also having five "prongs," they are broader on a sweet gum leaf. (Value range F).

Green River Formation landscape, Douglas Pass, Colorado.

Platanus leaf (California sycamore) extensively eaten by insects. Green River Formation, Douglas Pass, Colorado. (Value range F).

Three specimens of *Platanus wyomingensis (California sycamore)*, Green River Formation, Douglas Pass, Colorado. (Value range F, single specimen).

Platanus sp. leaf. Weathered at the top. Parachute Creek Member, Green River Formation, Bonanza, Utah.

Platanus sp. and Green River fish set in a bathroom wall along with tiles made of Neogene travertine.

Sweet gum(?) balls. Top: recent, bottom: fossil. Green River Formation, Bonanza, Utah.

Populus wilmattae. An early poplar. (Value range F).

Group of Green River leaves. Note that the majority of these leaves have smooth rims, a characteristic of warm climate (tropical) angiosperms. Top, bottom left, and bottom right: *Populus wilmattae*, upper right: *Cardiospermum* sp. (balloon vine). (Value range F, single leaf).

Cardiospermum coloradensis. Balloon vine, a tropical vine. Douglas Pass,
Colorado. (Value range F).

Beech (?). Moneta, Wyoming, Wasatch Formation.

Cardiospermum coloradensis. Balloon vine, Green River Formation, Bonanza, Utah.

Group of Green River leaves. Douglas Pass, Colorado.

Rhus nigricans, Bonanza, Utah. (Value range F).

Elongate leaf, Green River Formation. (Value range G).

Cercidiphyllum sp.,
Bonanza, Utah.

Flower, Green River Formation, Bonanza, Utah. (Value range F).

Eden Valley wood, Wyoming. Green River Formation. This petrified wood is quite popular with rockhounds and has been widely collected from the Lake Gosiute portion of the Green River Formation of western Wyoming. It is often made into bookends and even rounds of it are made into petrified wood clocks. (Value range F).

Yellowstone Hot Spot Volcanic Activity and Petrified Wood

Taxodium sp. Bald Cypress is a plant associated with warm climates. During the Eocene Epoch, Idaho was at a much lower elevation and the climate was sub-tropical. (Value range F).

The Yellowstone region of northwestern Wyoming represents what is known as a "hot spot" in the earth's mantle. This hot spot has been pumping out magma from the earth's mantle throughout much of the Cenozoic Era. In the early Cenozoic, specifically during the Eocene Epoch, this hot spot was underneath what is now Idaho and because North America has been moving westward as a consequence of continental drift, it has been moving over this hot spot, giving the appearance of the volcanic activity having moved progressively eastward. (Currently the hot spot is directly under Yellowstone Park). This volcanic activity throughout the Cenozoic has periodically buried forests with eruptions similar to those associated with Mt. St. Helens and has preserved the wood as petrified wood and the foliage as compressions in volcanic ash. These Eocene tuffs are especially well developed west of Yellowstone Park in Idaho.

Maple wood? Lakeview, Idaho. Eocene strata rich in volcanic ash containing petrified logs make up part of the Ranges west of Yellowstone Park. This region was over the "hot spot" during the Eocene, the North American continent having moved westward since that time while the hot spot remained stationary.

Eocene volcanoclastic sediments in Yellowstone Park containing petrified logs. The same volcanoclastic rocks make up Specimen Ridge where multiple erect logs of petrified trees are exposed along this stream.

Glyptostrobus sp. This is a common conifer in early Cenozoic rocks. This specimen is preserved in volcanic tuff from eruptions from the Yellowstone hot spot in Idaho during the Eocene Epoch. (Value range G).

Alaskan Eocene Leaves

Subtropical plants illustrated here come from coal bearing Eocene strata of southern Alaska. Early Cenozoic world climates generally were considerably warmer than are those of today and subtropical plants at that time appeared to have lived at high latitudes. (The Eocene has been considered to be one of the Earths warmest periods in its geologic past). Occurrences of tropical or subtropical fossil plants at high latitudes sometimes occur as a consequence of continental drift and/or sea floor spreading—a process which moves portions of the Earth's crust great distances and can place tropical fossils at high latitudes. In other cases tropical or subtropical plants in the northern hemisphere appear to have lived and thrived at latitudes as high as 70 degrees. Weather patterns now influenced by mountain ranges and other modern geography may have played a part in this, as before they existed, warm air masses were capable of traveling unimpeded to high latitudes. Coal beds, formed from the massive accumulation of these plants, are worked, sometimes at high latitudes, in Siberia as well as in Alaska. A major element of the Alaskan floras were primitive conifers such as *metasequoia and sequoia* as well as the bald cypress (*taxodium*), a conifer today associated with warm and wet climates.

The Mad Zoo, Valley Trash, and Eocene Fossil Plants!

The Palmer fossil plant flora occurs in an area north of Anchorage known as the Matanuska-Susitan Valley, locally referred as the "Mat-Su" valley. This is one of the more populated regions of Alaska and is currently characterized by some degree of urban sprawl spreading out from Anchorage. This region, the Mat-Su administrative borough, has been referred to by more affluent and erudite Alaskans as the "Mad-Zoo," and its occupants as "Valley Trash"—a rather unkind metaphor. The town of Wasilla, which is next to Palmer, has as its former mayor, Sarah Palin, formerly the governor of Alaska and a 2008 candidate for vice president of the US. What does such local bickering have to do with fossil plants? We have to go into this a little further. The largely evangelical community tarred as the "Valley Trash" of the "Mad Zoo" virtually ignores fossils, at best; however, if they can serve as an economic commodity in some way—for instance they might be sold to tourists (bona fide Alaskan fossils can be a desirable item with tourists)—then there would be an interest. The more "ivory tower," erudite crowd would say **no**, such fossils are a state and national treasure and it would be improper as well as illegal to sell them as some occur on federal land. The area around Palmer and Wasilla has been a coal mining area for decades with numerous pits and excavations dug into its tectonically deformed strata—some of these now overgrown excavations yield the subtropical fossil plants shown here. What is happening, though, is that reclamation of the old mines is not only tearing into vegetation that has grown on the pits (in many instances) for over fifty years but is also burying the greywacke slabs containing the fossils. Thus, this national and state treasure is being buried by "mine reclamation."

Coal and leaf bearing outcrop, Palmer, Alaska.

Outcrop in former coal mine with upright petrified tree (middle of picture), Eocene, Palmer, Alaska.

Which of the following two mindsets makes the most sense: the mindset of the Sarah Palin-evangelical-"valley trash" crowd who would deem it okay to leave the old mines alone and make a buck by selling the fossils but in not committing serious money to "reclaiming" well vegetated old coal pits or the politically correct crowd who abhor to see such "sacred" paleontological objects fall into the hands of tourists and collectors, but who seemingly **do approve** of the considerable costs involved in burying the fossils. The author believes that the former makes the most sense (and by the author's way of thinking would be the common sense approach); however, he has been informed by a member of the erudite, politically correct "establishment" that the concept of "**common sense** was invalid as it cannot be **legally defined.**"

Dipping (tilted) strata of leaf bearing outcrop, Eocene, Palmer, Alaska.

Sequoia sp. (redwood), Palmer, Alaska. (Value range F).

Two distinctive leaf types, Palmer, Alaska. (Value range E).

Populus sp. Poplar leaf, Palmer, Alaska.

Quercus sp., an oak.

74

Florissant Colorado Leaves

This Eocene (previous considered Lower Oligocene and even Miocene in earlier literature) flora and fauna has been beautifully preserved in volcanic ash beds (tuff) in the vicinity of Florissant, Colorado. These tuffs were deposited in volcanically formed lakes, which existed when parts of the Colorado Rockies were uplifting. The tuffs preserve, in an exquisite manner, an extensive flora of conifers and angiosperms, along with a diverse and abundant fauna of insects.

Bibliography

Berry, Edwin W. 1930. "Revision of the Lower Eocene Wilcox flora of the southeastern states with descriptions of new species, chiefly in Tennessee and Kentucky." *U.S. Geological Survey Professional Paper* 156.

Brown, Roland W. 1962. "Paleocene Flora of the Rocky Mountains and Great Plains." *U.S. Geological Survey Professional Paper* 375. Washington D.C.: U.S. Government Printing Office.

Kenrick, Paul and Paul Davis. 2004. *Fossil Plants*. Washington D.C. & London: Smithsonian Books and British Museum (Natural History).

Meyer, Herbert W. 2003. *The Fossils of Florissant*. Washington and London: Smithsonian Books.

Wittlake, Eugene B. 1968. "Fossil Mosses from the Upper Wilcox (Lower Eocene) of Arkansas." *The American Midland Naturalist* 80(2), pp. 543-547.

Large petrified stump (Sequoia or redwood) of the Colorado Petrified Forest, Florissant, Colorado. This was one of the highlights of the Petrified Forest. Volcanic tuff was dug away from the stump to expose it.

Group of additional Florissant, Colorado, leaves.

Excavation for fossil leaves and insects in Florissant tuffs, 1962.

Volcanic tuff exposure for collecting fossil leaves and insects at Colorado Petrified Forest, 1957. Now this area is covered and grassed over in Florissant Fossil Beds National Monument.

Group of Florissant, Colorado, leaves. (Value range D, for a group).

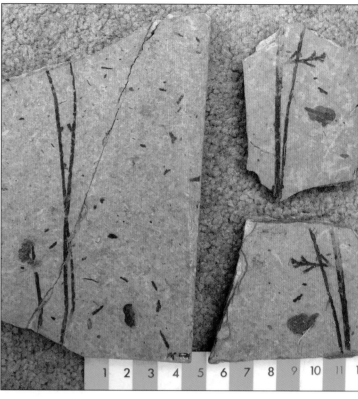

Pinus macqinitiel. Fossil pine needles look similar to those found today. (Value range F).

Metasequoia sp. are bald cypress, Florissant, Colorado.

Fagopsis longifolia. The most common leaf in the Florissant tuffs. (Value range F).

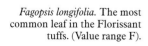

Two *Fagopsis* specimens collected at a pit that at the time was part of the Colorado Petrified Forest.

Robber fly and leaf, an extinct genus of elm (*Cedrelospermum lineatum*), Florissant tuff. (Value range E).

Chapter Three
Foraminifera, Corals, and Mollusks

Paleogene marine strata (limestone, marl, and shale) can locally be full of fossils. In many parts of the globe, marine Upper Cretaceous strata grade into strata of the Paleocene with the notable sharp disappearance of many invertebrates such as ammonites and belemnites as well as other mollusks. On the other hand, some mollusks such as *Turritella* continue right across the K/T boundary.

Large Foraminifera

Single celled organisms (foraminifera) which produced large tests (shells) are characteristic of the Paleogene. Foraminifers (forams) generally are considered to be microfossils and are useful in determining geologic horizons encountered in deep drilling by the petroleum industry. Most forams are so small that they can survive the trip up the drill stem and still be identified. Some Paleogene forams however are so large that they are in the same size range as mollusks. Such early Cenozoic foraminifera are some of the largest single celled organisms to have ever lived.

Lepidocyclina sp. The original name (Nummulites) for this large nummulit-id foram comes from its similarity in size and shape to a coin. Next to it at the bottom are two 2,000-year-old Roman coins and a U.S. quarter. Upper Eocene, Rohrdorf, North Germany.

Nummulites sp. These foraminifera resemble lentils. They come from a quarry in Eocene limestone that was used in construction of the Pyramids. Herodotus, a Greek philosopher of the 5th century B.C., thought that these lentil-shaped objects, which accumulate at the base of the pyramids, were petrified lentils from meals eaten by Egyptian slaves who built the pyramids. Eocene Limestone, Cairo, Egypt.

Lepidocyclina sp. A large nummulitid foraminifera which, like other similar forms resembles a coin. A 2,000+ year old, 2 cm Roman coin is shown for scale. Claiborne Group, Upper Eocene, St. Stephens, Alabama. (Value range F).

Sponges

Sponges that are readily recognizable, like this specimen, are desirable fossils.

Harpactocarcinus punctulatus. This interesting (and distinctive) sponge comes from Eocene strata near Verona, Italy. Lutetian age strata, Eocene. Avesa, Verona, Italy. (Value range E).

Corals

Corals of Cenozoic age can be attractive and locally abundant fossils.

Solitary corals. These solitary corals resemble (somewhat) the horn corals of the Paleozoic Era. Tallahatta Formation, Conecuh River, Covington County, Alabama. (Value range F, group of specimens).

Bryozoans

Bryozoans are conspicuous fossils in Paleozoic rocks. By contrast, they are not obvious fossils in Mesozoic and Cenozoic rocks.

Bryozoans. Eocene, Castle Rock Point Quarry, Castle Hayne, New Hannover, North Carolina.

Annelids

Calcareous tubes made by marine annelids (worms) are shown here. Similar worm tubes (and the worms that made them) are found in the shallow waters of modern oceans.

Outcrop of Ocala Limestone exposed along the Suwannee River showing the beds and the locality that produced the previously shown worm tubes.

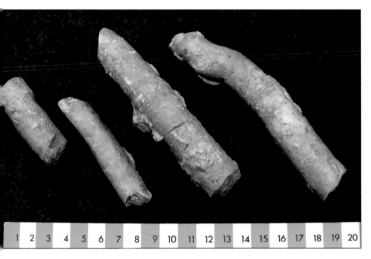

Worm tubes. Ocala Limestone, Suwannee River, northern Florida. (Value range F).

Brachiopod

Brachiopods, especially large ones like this, are rare fossils after the Paleozoic Era. A quantity of these specimens came onto the fossil market in the 1980s from an excavation in New Jersey.

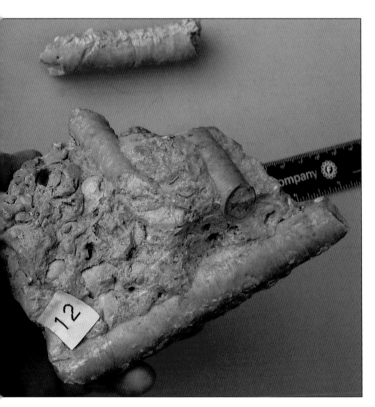

A worm tube in limestone matrix. Generally a fossil is more desirable when some of the rock matrix in which it was found is still present. Calcareous tubes are made by marine annelids. Ocala Limestone, Suwannee River, Florida.

Olenaothyris harlani. A particularly nice (and large) brachiopod from the Cenozoic Era, a relatively rare fossil in Cenozoic rocks. Eocene, New Egypt, New Jersey. (Value range F).

Mollusks-Pelecypods

Clams or Pelecypods are common fossils in Cenozoic marine rocks—they, like gastropods, are present in great variety in the Cenozoic.

Venericardia planicosta

Pelecypod

Eocene, Tuscahoma Fm.

Bell's Landing, Alabama R., Monroe Co., Alabama

Venericardia alticosta Conrad. This common (but fine) venus clam is characteristic of the Eocene, Jackson Group, White Bluff, Arkansas.

Venericardia planicosta. These lovely large Eocene venus clams come from Alabama. Tuscaloosa Formation, Bell Landing, Monroe County, Alabama. (Value range G).

Venericardia sp. Internal molds of a venus clam similar to that previously shown. Jackson Group, Dothan, Georgia. (Value range G).

Unio sp. A freshwater lake clam, from the Upper Eocene Green River Formation, Fossil Butte Member, Fossil, Wyoming. Beds of these fresh water clams preserving original nacre occur in the Green River Formation of "Fossil Lake" in Wyoming as well as elsewhere in the formation. (Value range F).

A fine clam! Jackson Group, White Bluff, Arkansas. (Value range G).

Freshwater clam similar to the previous example. This impression in burn-out from the Fort Union "Formation" was associated with impressions of fossil leaves. (Value range F).

Mollusks—Marine Gastropods

Marine and fresh water gastropods can be both attractive and common fossils in Paleogene rocks.

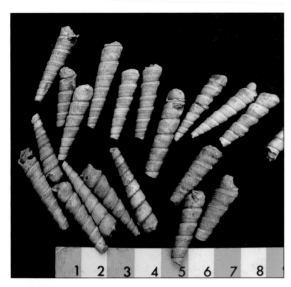

Turritella mortoni. Aquia Formation, Paleocene, King George County, Virginia. These gastropods occur in abundance either at the K/T (Cretaceous-Tertiary boundary) or just above it in large numbers over many parts of North America and elsewhere. Turritella's appear to have undergone a population explosion following the Cretaceous extinction event where strata can sometimes be full of them. (Value range F).

Turritella tremppina. Eocene, Tremp, Lleida, Spain. (Value range F for group).

Turritella sp. A silicified specimen from a large chert mass weathered from the Oligocene Marianna Limestone, Flint River, Georgia. (Value range F).

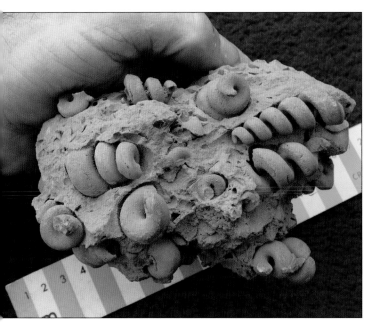

Internal molds of *Turritella mortoni*. Midway (Clayton Formation), low-ermost Paleocene or (possibly) latest Cretaceous. These fossils occur in abundance either at or just above the K-T boundary, which separates the Mesozoic Era from the Cenozoic. These large *Turritella* gastropods appear to have been immune to the event that caused the massive extinctions found at the K-T boundary. They occur, often in large quantity, just above the extinction event. These came from outcrops near Possum Grape, Arkansas.

Turritella pachecoensis. Paleocene Epoch, Pozo Formation, Santa Cruse Island, California. These turritellas come from a zone of strata at or just above the K-T boundary. They come from a widespread horizon (population explosion?) of this high-spired gastropod just after the K-T extinction event. Pozo Formation, Paleocene, Santa Cruz Islands, California. (Value range F).

Turritella mortoni. Internal molds of this lowermost Cenozoic gastropod. These are of the same age as the previous specimens from Arkansas. Aquia Formation, Potomac River, Maryland. Internal molds like these from the Aquia Formation have been widely distributed through fossil collectors and dealers. (Value range F).

Conus sp. Jackson Group, Eocene, Brazos River, Texas. This is a species of gastropod common in modern seas. Here is one of its earliest occurrences of what today are known as cone shells. (Value range G).

Left: *Turritella*-like; middle: *Strobus* sp.; right: a welk. Claiborne Group, Clairborne, Alabama.

89

of the constituent rocky masses now entering into the centra
ridges of these chains had been deposited in the sea.

The marine shells of the London clay confirm the inferenc

SHELLS OF THE LONDON CLAY.

The London Clay, an Eocene formation that underlies London, England, contains a marine fauna similar to that of the Paris Basin. Here is a plate illustrating London Clay snails from Charles Lyell's *Elements of Geology*, 1865. Eocene strata at Clairborne, Alabama, were found by Lyell to yield a molluscan fauna quite similar to that of the London clay.

Fig. 207.

Voluta nodosa,
Sow. Highgate.

Fig. 208.

Phorus extensus,
Sow. Highgate.

Fig. 209.

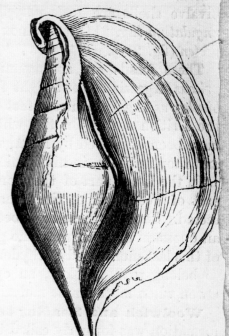

Rostellaria (Hippocrenes) ampla, Brander
$\frac{1}{3}$ of nat. size; also found in the Barton clay.

Fig. 210.

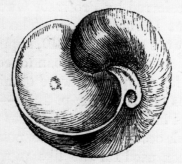

Nautilus centralis, Sow. Highgate.

Fig. 211.

a   b

Aturia ziczac, Bronn. Syn. *Nautilus
ziczac,* Sow. London clay. Sheppey.

Fig. 212.

Belosepia sepioidea, De Blainv.
London clay. Sheppey.

Fig. 213.

Leda amygdaloides
Sow. Highgate.

Fig. 214.

*Cryptodon (Axinus)
angulatum,* Sow.
London clay. Hornsey.

Fig. 215.

Astropecten crispatus,
E. Forbes. Sheppey.

M

Freshwater Gastropods

Freshwater gastropods lived in large numbers in the lakes where the Green River Formation was deposited. Rocks composed of the shells of these mollusks are popular with rock hounds, who use them to make agate jewelry, bookends, and even the facings of clocks. Freshwater mollusks (particularly gastropods) are also sometimes found associated with a distinctive type of limestone known as travertine. Travertine is formed from the deposits of lime charged springs, often geothermal or hot springs.

Cerithium sp. Turitella-like fresh water gastropod. These gastropods are preserved in travertine, a type of limestone deposited by springs and of freshwater origin. Travertine has a distinctive appearance; it is usually somewhat porous and found associated with modern or ancient springs, sometimes of hot or geothermal origin. These gastropods are not of the genus *Turritella*, as that is a marine genus—they are fresh water snails from near Paris, France. (Value range G).

Freshwater snails preserved in travertine, Paris Basin. Strata of the Paris Basin contain freshwater layers, sometimes made up of this spring deposited limestone, which can locally be full of these freshwater gastropods.

2. Next below are freshwater and estuary marls and carbonaceous clays, in the brackish-water portion of which are found abundantly *Cerithium plicatum*, Lam. (fig. 160), *C. elegans* (fig. 161), and *C. tricinctum* ; also *Rissoa Chastelii* (fig. 162), a very

Fig. 160. Fig. 161. Fig. 162. Fig. 163.

Cerithium plicatum, Lam. Hempstead. | *Cerithium elegans*. Hempstead. | *Rissoa Chastelii*, Nyst, Sp. Hempstead, Isle of Wight. | *Paludina lenta*. Hempstead Bed.

common Kleyn Spawen shell, and which occurs in each of the four subdivisions of the Hempstead series down to its base, where it passes into the Bembridge beds. In the freshwater portion of the same beds *Paludina lenta* (fig. 163) occurs ; a shell identified by some conchologists with a species now living, *P. unicolor*; also several species of *Lymneus*, *Planorbis*, and *Unio*.

Presented here is a discussion by Charles Lyell on brackish and freshwater snails of the Paris Basin, snails similar to those shown previously.

Calcaire siliceux, or Travertin inférieur (A. 2 and 3, p. 227).—This compact siliceous limestone extends over a wide area. It resembles a precipitate from the waters of mineral springs, and is often traversed by small empty sinuous cavities. It is, for the most part, devoid of organic remains, but in some places contains freshwater and land species, and never any marine fossils. The calcaire siliceux and the calcaire grossier usually occupy distinct parts of the Paris basin, the one attaining its fullest development in those places where the other is of slight thickness. They are described by some writers as alternating with each other towards the centre of the basin, as at Sergy and Osny.

The gypsum, with its associated marls before described, is in greatest force towards the centre of the basin, where the calcaire grossier and calcaire siliceux are less fully developed.

Charles Lyell's discussion of travertine in *Elements of Geology*, 1865.

Travertine facing on a wall: This limestone, with its distinctive texture, is often cut and polished and used as ornamental rock facing on the interiors of buildings. Here is a lobby wall faced with travertine from Wyoming.

"Turritella" agate (*Oxyterma* sp.), Green River Formation, south of Wamsutter, Sweetwater County, Wyoming. The gastropods in this popular rockhound material are **not** Turritella, which is a **marine gastropod**. The fossils in this silicified rock are **fresh water snails**, which lived in a large lake! (Value range G).

Oreoconus sp. Fresh water gastropods of the Green River Formation, Baggs, Wyoming. These freshwater gastropods locally occur in abundance in the freshwater lake deposits of the Green River Formation of Wyoming and Colorado. (Value range H).

Goniobasis tenera (Hall). Oncolite formed around a fresh water snail, Green River Formation, Wyoming. The bands of material around this fresh water gastropod were formed (precipitated) by cyanobacteria (blue-green algae) living in a large, fresh water lake (Lake Uinta) in which the Green River Formation was deposited. Such a concretionary buildup of mineral matter by microbes is known as an oncolite and is related to a stromatolite. Stromatolites are the oldest known fossils, some going back to the earliest history of life, some 3.5 billion years. (Value range G).

More of the genus *Oxyterma* sp. Chunks of "Turritella" agate, Green River Formation. This is a popular material for working into bookends, jewelry, and other decorative items by rockhounds.

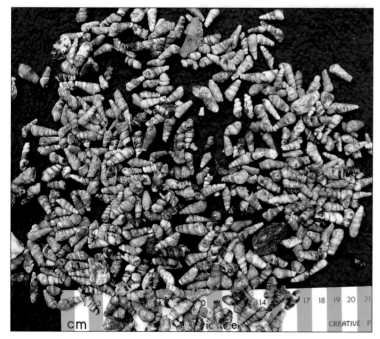

Oxyterma sp. Loose "Turritella" specimens, Green River Formation. These fresh water snails are **not** of the genus Turritella—that is a name given to them by rockhounds. Turritella is a marine gastropod genus; these are from the fresh water Green River Formation of Upper Eocene age (Lake Uinta). (Value range F for group).

Land snails. Oligocene Brule Formation, Badlands, South Dakota. (Value range H).

Mollusks—Cephalopods

Coiled cephalopods, similar to the modern coiled nautilus, are found in Cenozoic strata, but the straight cephalopods and the ammonites, so abundant in the Paleozoic and Mesozoic Eras respectively are gone in the Cenozoic Era.

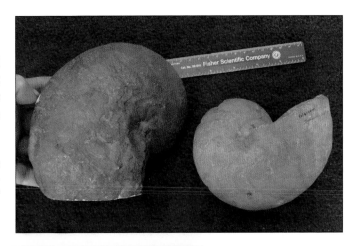

Another group of *Hercoglossa ulrichi* from west of Clairborne, Alabama. (Value range F, single specimen).

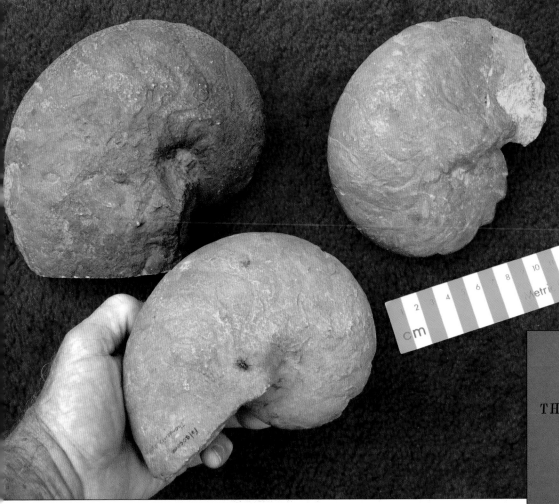

Hercoglossa ulrichi. A nautaloid characteristic of the Paleocene Epoch. These nautaloids have a somewhat undulating suture pattern. They come from a zone underneath strata exposed along the Alabama River near Claiborne, Alabama (Claiborne Group), which was a locality visited (and collected) by Charles Lyell in 1846 on his second visit to the "United States of North America." (Value range F).

Frontispiece of Lyell's account of 1846-47, "A Second Visit to the United States of North America," published in 1849. In this work, Charles Lyell gives accounts of collecting Eocene fossils at Clairborne bluff on the Alabama River. The previously illustrated nautaloids (*Hercoglossa ulrichi*) came from strata beneath the Eocene strata at Claiborne bluff. Lyell was unaware of these nautaloids. They were discovered sixty years after Lyell's visit by E.O. Ulrich, an early twentieth century stratigrapher-paleontologist known for his proposal of the Ozarkian Period—a geologic period to be placed between the Cambrian and the Ordovician periods of the Paleozoic era. The species is named after Ulrich.

A SECOND VISIT

TO

THE UNITED STATES

OF

NORTH AMERICA.

BY

SIR CHARLES LYELL, F.R.S.

PRESIDENT OF THE GEOLOGICAL SOCIETY OF LONDON,
AUTHOR OF "THE PRINCIPLES OF GEOLOGY,"
AND "TRAVELS IN NORTH AMERICA."

IN TWO VOLUMES.

VOL. I.

LONDON:
JOHN MURRAY, ALBEMARLE STREET.
1849.

In the course of the night we were informed that the Amaranth had reached Claiborne. Here we found a flight of wooden steps, like a ladder, leading up the nearly perpendicular bluff, which was 150 feet high. By the side of these steps was a framework of wood, forming the inclined plane down which the cotton bales were lowered by ropes. Captain Bragdon politely gave his arm to my wife, and two negroes preceded us with blazing torches of pine-wood, throwing their light on the bright shining leaves of several splendid magnolias which covered the steep. We were followed by a long train of negroes, each carrying some article of our baggage. Having ascended the steps, we came to a flat terrace, covered with grass, the first green sward we had seen for many weeks, and found there a small, quiet inn, where we resolved to spend some days, to make a collection of the fossil tertiary shells, so well known to geologists as abounding in the strata of this cliff. About 400 species, belonging to the Eocene formation, derived from this classic ground, have already been named, and they agree, some of

Claiborne, Alabama, was a steamboat landing on the Alabama River. High ground outcrops, like the Claiborne Bluff, were particularly useful for landings, especially during periods of high water. Here is Lyell's description of the locality in 1846, which was visited and collected by the author 120 years later.

Echinoderms—Echinoids

Echinoids (sea urchins) can be common fossils in early Cenozoic strata. Other echinoderm classes like crinoids and asteroids (starfish) generally are rare fossils in Cenozoic strata.

Bibliography

British Museum. 1975. *British Caenozoic Fossils*. London: British Museum (Natural History).

Brown, Robin C. 1988. *Florida's Fossils, Guide to Location, Identification, and Enjoyment*. Sarasota, Florida: Pineapple Press.

Nautaloid. Eocene, western Washington State. This is an Eocene nautaloid similar to those from near Claiborne, Alabama, but coming from Eocene rocks deposited in the eastern Pacific. (Value range F).

Amblypygus americanus. Very fine sea urchins! Upper Eocene, Crystal River, Lafayette, County, Florida. (Value range F, for all five urchins).

Ryncholampas carolinensis. Castle Hayne Formation, Rockport, New Hanover County, North Carolina. (Value range G).

Periarchus lyelli, An echinoid species named after Charles Lyell. Castle Hayne Formation, New Hanover County, Castle Hayne, North Carolina. (Value range F).

Hardouinia kellumi. Castle Hayne Formation, New Hanover, North Carolina. (Value range G).

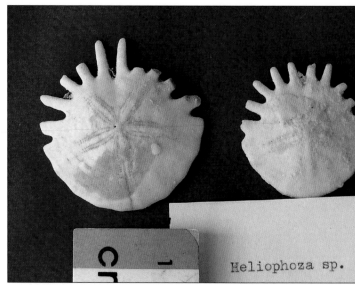

Heliophoza sp. (Sand dollar) with spines. Oligocene, Morocco. (Value range F).

Cassidulus (Paralampus) globosus. Moody's Branch Formation, Eocene, Withlacochee River, Levy County, Florida. (Value range G).

Rotoloidea sp. Sand dollar with spikes at the end. Eocene, Morocco. (Value range F).

Rhyncholampas gouldi. Oligocene, Suwannee Formation,
Brooksville, Hernando County, Florida. (Value range G).

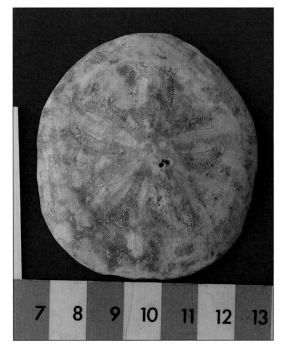

Clypeaster rogersi (Morton). Mariana Limestone, Oligocene,
Castleberry, Conecuh County, Alabama. (Value range G).

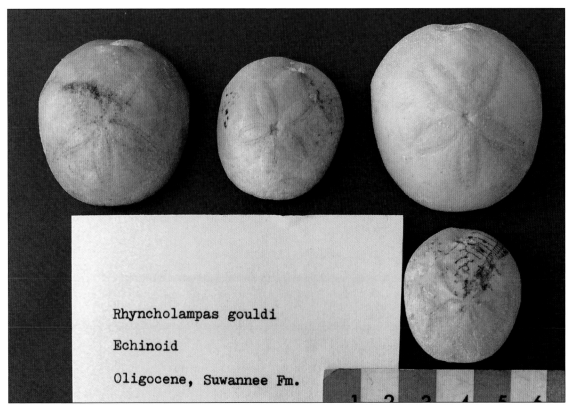

Rhyncholampas gouldi.
Suwannee Formation,
Oligocene, Brooks-
ville, Hernando
County, Florida.
(Value range F).

Lithina sp. Paleocene, Furman, Wilcox County, Alabama. This is a small, distinctive echinoid that survived the Mesozoic extinction event. (Value range G).

Oligopygus whetherbyi. Crystal River Formation, Upper Eocene, Mayo, Lafayette County, Florida. (Value range H).

Cassidulus gouldi. Suwannee Formation, Suwannee River, Hamilton, Suwannee County, Florida. (Value range H).

Schizaster araiger. Marianna Limestone, Oligocene, Perdue Hill, Monroe County, Alabama. (Value range G).

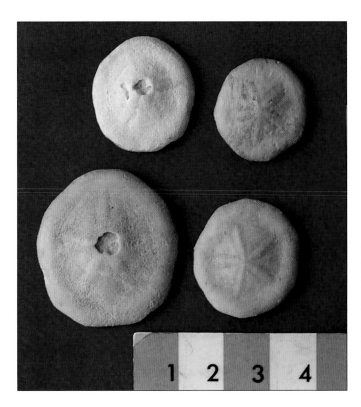

Neolaganum durhami. Crystal River Formation, Upper Eocene, Suwannee County, Florida.

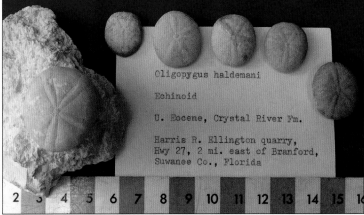

Oligopygus haldamani. Crystal River Formation, Suwannee County, Florida. (Value range G).

Neolaganum durhami. Crystal River Formation, Upper Eocene, Suwannee County, Florida.

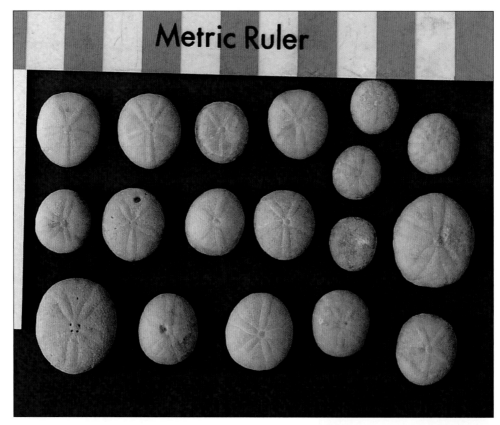

Oligopygus haldamani. Crystal River Formation, Upper Eocene, Suwannee County, Florida. (Value range G).

Phymotoxis mansfieldi. This is an example of a regular urchin. Most Eocene and Oligocene sea urchins are irregular urchins; they have bilateral rather than radial symmetry, as does this genus. Suwannee Formation, Oligocene, Brooksville, Hernando County, Florida. (Value range F).

Cassidulus globosus. Crystal River Formation, Upper Eocene, Lafayette County, Florida.

Eupatagus mooreanus. This is a nice group of these irregular urchins from the Eocene of Florida. Echinoids of the genus
Eupatagus have been widely dispersed among collectors and are one of the most commonly seen fossil urchins from Florida.
Moody's Branch Formation, Inglis, Florida. (Value range G, single specimen).

Euptagus mooreanus. Here is another group of echinoids from the Eocene
of Florida, echinoids that have been widely distributed among collectors.
Moody's Branch Formation, Inglis, Florida.

Echinocyamus ovatus Munster. An irregular urchin from Paleogene strata
of northern Europe. Oligocene, Doberg/Bunde, northern Germany.
(Value range F).

Rhyncholampas gouldi. A group of chert steinkerns of this common Oligocene echinoid. These are found in boulders of flint or chert which weather from the Ocala Limestone of northern Florida. Suwannee River, northern Florida. (Value range E, for a group).

Oligopygus whetherbyi

Echinoid

U. Eocene, Crystal River Fm.

NB & A Lime Rock Co. quarry,

Oligopygus whetherbyi. Upper Eocene, Crystal River Formation, Suwannee County, Florida.

Eupatagus mooreanus. Eocene, Moody's Branch Formation, Inglis, Florida. This is another group of nice fossil urchins, which have been widely distributed among fossil collectors. (Value range G, single specimen).

cm

3 4

Chapter Four

Crustaceans, Insects, and Arachnids

Crabs and Lobsters

Fossil crabs and lobsters are some of the more collectable fossils, being relatively rare but not so rare that they are seldom seen. Often they occur enclosed in concretions or nodules like those shown here. When broken open with a hammer or by the freeze thaw cycle, they can reveal the crustaceans, spread out claws, pincers, and all. Such fossils in concretions have been collectable for hundreds of years. Eighteenth and nineteenth century authors often referred to occurrences of fossils like these as being placed in "little coffins." They were also known in those centuries as "medals of creation."

Zanthopsis (Pualius) vulgaris. This is a lovely fossil crab; however, I do wonder what it is that is vulgar about it? Lincoln Creek, Oligocene, Wahiakum County, southwestern Washington.

Megokus macropinus. A small (but nice) crab preserved in a nodule. Late Eocene, Quinper Formation, Jefferson County, Washington. (Value range F)

1 2 3 4 5 6 7 8 9 10 11 12 13

Zanthopsis (Pualius) vulgaris. Another nice (but vulgar?) fossil crab. Lincoln Creek, Oligicene, Wahiakum County, southwestern Washington state.

7 8 9 10 11 12 13 14 15 16 17 18 19 20 21

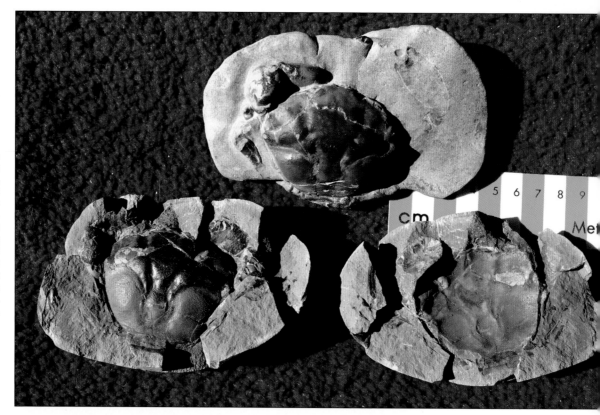

Zanthopsis vulgaris. These crabs occur in nodules or concretions, a common preservation phenomenon with fossil crabs and lobsters. The concretions erode from soft shale and are split open and revealed by the freeze-thaw cycle. Lincoln Creek Formation, Wahiakum County, Washington. (Value range F).

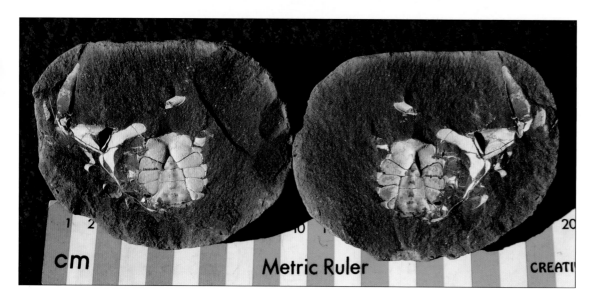

Zanthopsis vulgaris Rathbun. Incomplete crab specimen, but otherwise well preserved in a hard calcareous concretion. Lincoln Creek Formation, Late Eocene, Wahiakum County, Washington.

Branchioplax washingtoniana Rathbun. A sharp, well preserved crab symmetrically placed in its concretion. Hoko Formation, Clallam County, Washington state. (Value range E)

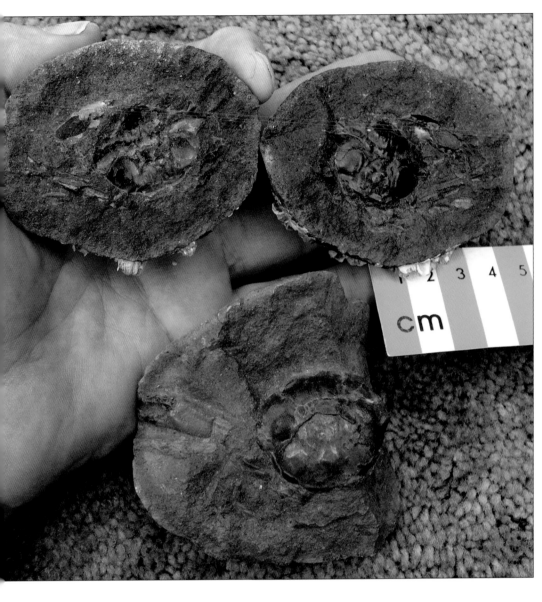

Branchioplax washingtoniana
Rathbun. Hoko Formation,
Clallam County, Washington state.

This is a crab bearing concretion with modern barnacles on the surface. These fossil crabs are sometimes found in concretions that erode from the sea cliffs of western Washington. They are, as this one was, collected from beaches or in shallow water adjacent to the beach.

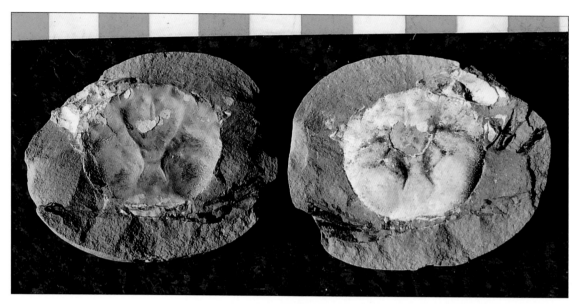

Portunites alaskensis Rathbun. Lincoln Creek Formation, Oligocene Epoch, Grays Harbor County, Washington.

Portunites triangulum. Lincoln Creek Formation, Oligocene, southwestern Washington state.

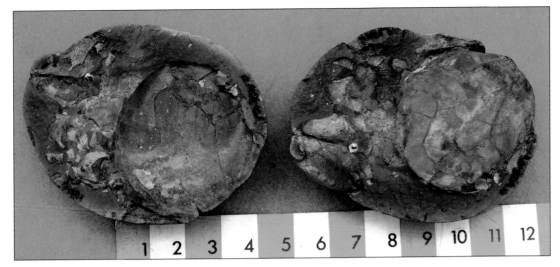

Unidentified crab. Upper Eocene, Jackson Group, Brazos River, Texas. These crabs are preserved in concretions that erode from bluffs along the Brazos River and its tributaries. (Value range F).

Necronectes vaughani. Glendon Limestone, Lower Oligocene. Clairborne, Alabama. (Value range E).

Lobster claw. Claiborne Group, Upper Eocene outcrops along the Tombigbee River, St. Stephens, Alabama. (Value range F).

Plocoscyphia sp. Here is a spiffy, small complete crab from Oligocene beds. Chiampo, Vicenza, Italy. (Value range D).

Plocoscyphia sp. Another view of the above, delightful fossil crab. Note the black color of its pincers—original pigment preservation. Chiampo, Vicenza, Italy.

Lobocarcinus paulino-wurtemburgensis Meyer. A nice crab from Eocene Limestone quarried in the vicinity of Cairo, Egypt. (Value range E).

Insects
—Green River Formation

Certain layers in the previously mentioned Green River Formation, a predominantly fresh water limestone deposited in large Eocene lakes of Wyoming, Utah, and Colorado, can yield abundant fossil insects and their larva. Insects, on falling into the Green River lakes, could be quickly covered by accumulating fine sediment, which included fine-grained volcanic ash. Besides its well-known fossil fish, insects are probably the second most desirable common fossils of the Green River Formation.

Plecia pealei. Two March flies—same as in the previous photo.

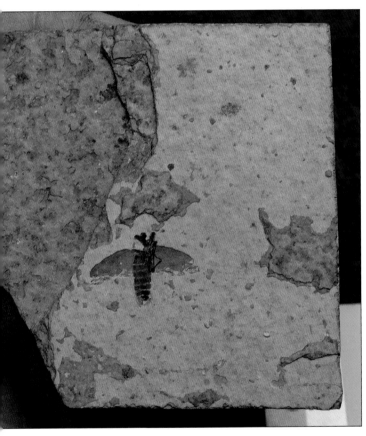

Plecia pealei. A March fly, Green River Formation, Fossil Butte Member, Kemmerer, Wyoming. (Value range E).

Plecia pealei. Two March flies on a slab of oil shale. Fossil Butte Member, Green River Formation. (Value range E).

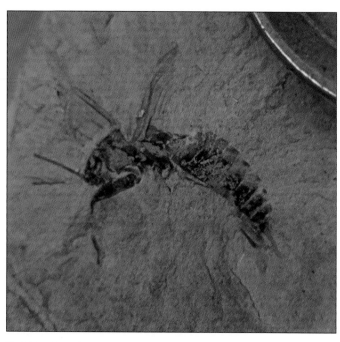

Bee? Parachute Creek Member, Green River Formation, Douglas Pass, Colorado.

March Fly—wings folded back on itself. Fossil Butte Member, Green River Formation. (Value range E).

Pronophlebia redivivi. Crain fly. Parachute Creek Member, Green River Formation, Douglas Pass, Colorado.

Pronophlebia sp. Crain fly. Part and counterpart. Parachute Creek Member, Green River Formation, Douglas Pass, Colorado. (Value range F).

Tipula sp. Crain fly. Antero Formation, Oligocene, Hartsel, Colorado. From a Neogene lake deposit similar to the Green River Formation but much more localized.

Lithophypoderma sp. Part of a mass mortality layer of bott fly larva from Lake Uinta sediments (Parachute Creek Member), Douglas Pass, Colorado. (Value range F).

Lithophypoderma sp. Bott fly larva. Parachute Creek Member, Green River Formation. (Value range F).

Insects—Florissant, Colorado

Volcanic activity during the Eocene and Oligocene epochs accompanying the uplift of the Rocky Mountains resulted in the fall of fine volcanic ash into nearby lakes and lagoons formed from streams dammed by volcanic activity. This ash-fall was slow and gentle so that leaves falling or floating on a lagoon's surface would be gently buried by the accumulating ash, thus preserving them. Associated with this scenario was the growth of large numbers of diatoms encouraged to flourish from the silica coming from the volcanic activity. These volcanic ash beds (tuffs) and associated diatoms buried a myriad of insects flying over the lagoons when ash was falling or it buried insects which fell into the lagoons—the end result was sending them to the bottom of the lagoon to be buried by the fine ash. Part of the outcrop area of the Florissant tuffs has become the site of toney mountain **developments**. Another portion has been saved from land development and is now the Florissant Fossil Beds National Monument, which is off limits to collecting. Currently one fee site is available for limited collecting.

Robber fly. Florissant tuff, Late Eocene, Florissant, Colorado. (Value range E).

Tipula heilprini. (Crain fly). Florissant Tuff, Late Eocene, Florissant, Colorado.

Lacewing.

Arachnid, Spider

Here is an example of a fossilized spider from Florissant, Colorado.

Hover fly?

Spider. Spiders are not insects! They often are found with fossil insects, as they were (and still are) predators of insects. This is a fossil spider preserved in the Florissant tuffs.

Bug! Florissant Tuffs, Florissant, Colorado.

Insects in Amber

Early Cenozoic amber containing insect inclusions occur at a number of localities around the globe. The best-known occurrence is found in the Baltic Sea area of northern Europe where amber has been gathered for many hundreds of years. Baltic amber has a cachet of value and respectability and its insect inclusions are some of the nicest to be found anywhere, although they are generally small. Fossil inclusions in amber of Paleogene age also occur in amber from the Dominican Republic. Dominican amber ranges in age from Eocene to Miocene, but generally it's difficult to determine its precise geologic age as the epochs themselves were based upon marine faunas. Fossils found as inclusions in amber are of terrestrial animals and this makes dating more challenging.

Less well known is the Oligocene amber from Simojovel in the southern Mexican state of Chiapas. Paleogene amber carrying insects and other inclusions is also known from southeastern Asia. It is a good possibility that other sources of Paleogene amber may turn up in the future and go on the gem and fossil market. With insects in amber two separate markets intersect, the gem market and the fossil market. The former market is generally the more lucrative monetarily and is the one that usually wins out when the two compete.

It should be mentioned that all early Cenozoic fossil resins are usually true amber—younger fossil resins that might be referred to as amber would be more accurately referred to as "copalite." Amber is a relative hard material and is not prone to crazing (developing small cracks over time) as are the geologically younger fossil resins like copalite.

Bibliography

Meyer, Herbert W. 2003. *The Fossils of Florissant*. Washington and London: Smithsonian Books.

Poinar, Jr., George O. 1992. *Life in Amber*. Stanford, California: Stanford University Press.

Rathbun, Mary J. 1935. "Fossil Crustacea of the Atlantic and Gulf Coastal Plain." *Geological Society of America. Special Paper 2*.

Rice, Patty C. 1980. *Amber, the Golden Gem of the Ages*. Van Nostrand Reinhold Company.

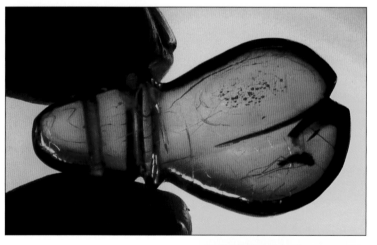

Mosquito in amber. Simojovel, Chiapus, southern Mexico. Local Indians work this amber. Chiapas amber has been placed both in the Oligocene and in the Miocene. The precise geological age of amber is often difficult to determine as amber sometimes has been reworked from earlier deposits.

Large mosquito-like insect. Dominican amber. (Value range E).

Insect inclusions in amber. Oligocene, Dominican Republic. Dominican amber is one of the most prolific amber occurrences that contain insect inclusions. Dominican amber comes from various stratigraphic horizons in the mountains of the eastern part of the island of Hispaniola. It ranges in age from Eocene to Miocene, depending upon the locality where it was mined.

Ants in Baltic amber. Eocene.
(Value range D).

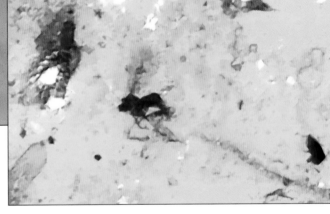

Small fly. Dominican Amber, Oligocene.

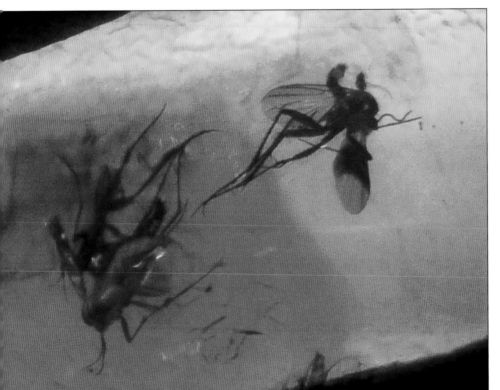

Fly and cricket in Baltic amber.
(Value range E).

Chapter Five
Sharks, Rays, and Fish

Sharks

Shark's teeth can be some of the most common Cenozoic fossils, sometimes being more abundant than those of invertebrates like mollusks and corals. Some of the most spectacular shark's teeth on the fossil market come from Paleocene (Paleocene and Eocene) phosphate mines in southeastern Morocco. Many of these teeth are large and well preserved, while the smaller ones can be exceedingly abundant and have entered the fossil market in vast numbers, where they are popular with children.

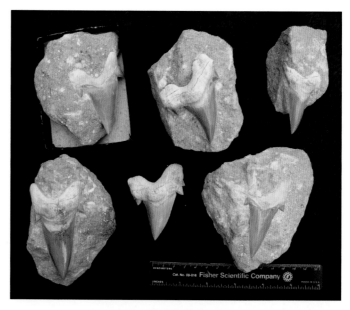

Lamna (obliqua) bicuspida. Numerous, excellent large shark teeth have come from phosphate mines in southwestern Morocco. Most of these teeth belong to the shark genus Lamna and most appear to be Eocene in age. The Moroccan phosphate rock ranges from Upper Cretaceous through the Paleocene into the Eocene Epoch so that the phosphate bearing beds span the K-T boundary. (Value range F, single tooth).

Odontaspis sp. Goblin shark teeth. This is a group of shark's teeth from the northern end of the Gulf embayment. Clayton Formation, Paleocene, Ardeola, Missouri. (Value range F for group).

Lamna sp. Two typical well-preserved shark teeth from phosphate rock, southwestern Morocco. Khouribga, Morocco.

Odontaspis sp. A group of goblin shark teeth from Crowley's Ridge, Jackson Group, Forrest City, Arkansas. (Value range F for group).

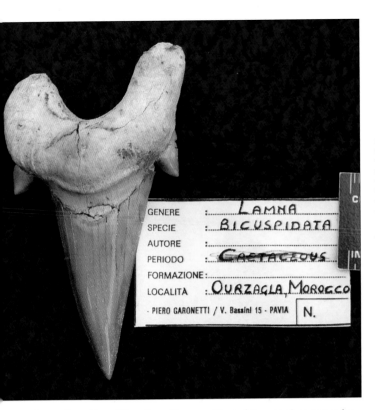

Lamna bicuspidata. Khouribga, Morocco. Most of these teeth appear to be either Paleocene or Eocene, although the Moroccan phosphate deposits range in age from Late Cretaceous to Eocene and span the K-T boundary. This specimen was originally labeled as being from the Cretaceous, however it is probably either Paleocene or Eocene in age. The Moroccan phosphate deposits span the K/T boundary, but these large shark teeth appear to be more common in Cenozoic rocks.

Stingrays

Fossil ray teeth are often found associated with those of sharks and like shark's teeth can be very common locally in Cenozoic marine strata. Much rarer are complete stingray specimens, the best-known early Cenozoic occurrences being those from lower beds of the Green River Formation of western Wyoming. The Green River Formation is normally thought of as a fresh or brackish water series of lake deposits; however, its earlier beds had some connection to the sea allowing rays to enter the lake system, particularly that lake which existed in the area of what is now western Wyoming and known as "Fossil Lake."

Three regions or lakes were the site of deposition of the Green River Formation: Fossil Lake, the smallest one and the source of the majority of Green River fish; Lake Gosiute south of Fossil Lake; and the largest one, Lake Uinta of Utah and western Colorado. These large and usually shallow lakes existed in a tropical or subtropical climate, in the environment of the Eocene Epoch.

Hemipristus sp. Upper jaw tooth. Eocene, Aquia Marl, Potomac Creek, Virginia.

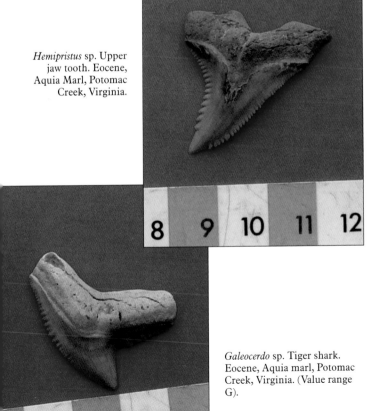

Galeocerdo sp. Tiger shark. Eocene, Aquia marl, Potomac Creek, Virginia. (Value range G).

Stingray teeth. Typical fossil ray teeth from a marine environment. Jackson Group, Crowley's Ridge, Forrest City, Arkansas. In marine formations this is what is usually found of stingrays, unlike those found in brackish water or lagoon environments where complete specimens can occur. (Value range F, for group).

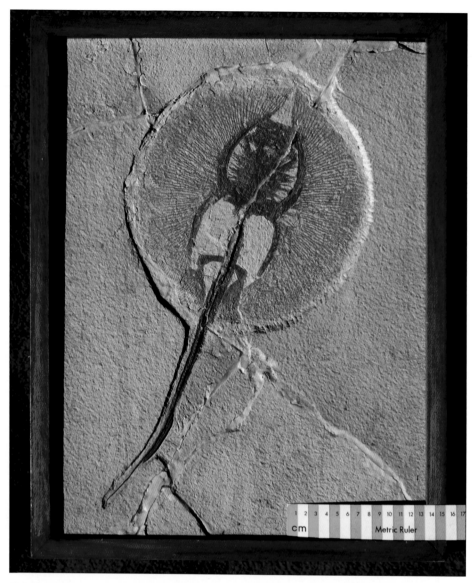

Heliobatis radians Marsh 1977. A brackish water or freshwater stingray. Fossil Butte Member, Green River Formation. These rays come from layers deposited in brackish water of the lower portion of the Green River Formation, Fossil Lake Member in western Wyoming. (Value range D).

Heliobatus radians Marsh 1877. A stingray collected in the 1920s from the Fossil Butte Member, Green River Formation. *Courtesy of Washington University Dept. of Earth and Planetary Sciences.*

Green River Formation

The Eocene Green River Formation covers a large portion of western Wyoming, northern Utah, and western Colorado. It was deposited in a series of three lakes and now includes thick layers of petroliferous shale or oil shale. For over a century efforts have been made to mine and process this hard, black rock as a source of petroleum—the most recent major activity of this sort being in the late 1970s. Fossils are found sporadically throughout the Formation; however, the best and most abundant fossils come from the aforementioned Fossil Lake deposits of western Wyoming.

Fish bearing strata of the Fossil Butte Member of the Green River Formation (Fossil Lake deposits), 1961.

Fossil Butte as it appeared in 1961.

The same outcrop as shown in the previous picture. The small building in the foreground is a sheep shelter used for grazing sheep in the area before it became a national monument.

Roadside sign explaining the geology of Fossil Butte, which is the butte seen in the background, 1961.

Distant view of Fossil Butte near Kemmerer, Wyoming, western Wyoming.

Green River Fossil Fish

Green River fossil fish were first noted in the late 1860s during the construction of the Union Pacific railroad across southwest Wyoming near the Green River, a major tributary of the Colorado. Shortly after this discovery, the fossil fish occurrence at Fossil Butte west of Kemmerer, Wyoming, was discovered; many of the fish found there were described by Edwin Drinker Cope of dinosaur fame and one of the players in the Cope and Marsh debacle.

Mioplosus labracoides Cope. A relatively common fish from the fossil lake deposits near Fossil, Wyoming. (Value range E).

Diplomystus dentatus. A bony (teleost fish) from Eocene lake deposits of the Green River Formation of the Fossil Lake occurrence. *Diplomystus* is one of the larger fish found in the Fossil Butte—Kemmerer, Wyoming, area. *Courtesy of Dept. of Earth and Planetary Sciences, Washington University, St. Louis.*

Prisicara serrata Cope. A bass, a relatively common predaceous fish of the Green River Formation of the Fossil Lake deposits and Fossil Butte near Fossil, Wyoming. (Value range E).

Phareodus testis Cope. A less frequently seen species of bass. Many of the Fossil Butte fishes were described by Edwin Drinker Cope (of dinosaur fame) in the 1870s. Fossil Butte Member, Kemmerer, Wyoming. (Value range E).

Prisicara serrata Cope. Another nice specimen of this predaceous fish from Fossil Butte preserved in a hard limestone. The black objects above the fish are fish coprolites. (Value range F).

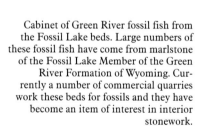

Cabinet of Green River fossil fish from the Fossil Lake beds. Large numbers of these fossil fish have come from marlstone of the Fossil Lake Member of the Green River Formation of Wyoming. Currently a number of commercial quarries work these beds for fossils and they have become an item of interest in interior stonework.

Asineops squamiforons Cope. (Donkey face fish). Lake Gosiute, Laney Member, Sweetwater County, Wyoming. (Value range D, rare).

Phareodus testes Cope. (Value range E).

Mioplosus labracoides Cope. (Value range F, has visible cracks).

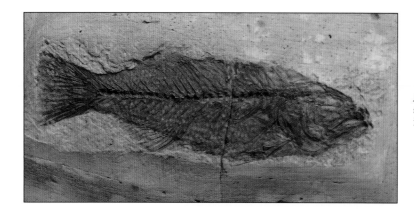

Mioplosus labracoides Cope. Another specimen of this distinctive Green River fish. (Value range F, repaired).

School of herrings. Note how pigmented eyes are preserved as dark specks. This appears to be a residue of redopsin—the visual pigment in the vertebrate eye. (Value range E).

Green River fossil fish (and leaves) set as tiles with travertine tiles on a bathroom wall. Is the kitty interested in a *Mioplosus* fish dinner?

Lepisosteus sp. Gar. Gar pikes can be common fossils in early Cenozoic deposits, but generally are very fragmentary. This is a gar preserved in oil shale from the Green River Formation of central Utah, the Lake Unita deposits—a thick sequence of oil shale which from time to time has been prospected and tested as a source for petroleum. Oil shale zones of the Green River Formation generally yield few fossils and those that are present, like this gar, are difficult to see and remove from this hard rock. (Value range E).

Gosiutichthys parvus. A large number of slabs covered by this herring came from road excavations near La Barge, Lincoln County, Wyoming. These are from and named after the Lake Gosiute portion of the Green River Formation. (Value range E).

Knightia sp. Mortality slab. A number of large slabs of these fish came from excavations near Fontenelle, Wyoming, from horizons of the Green River Formation not usually known to produce fossil fish. (Value range D).

Flip side of the same slab as shown above with compressions of Knightia on the bedding plane below that yielding those of the previous photo.

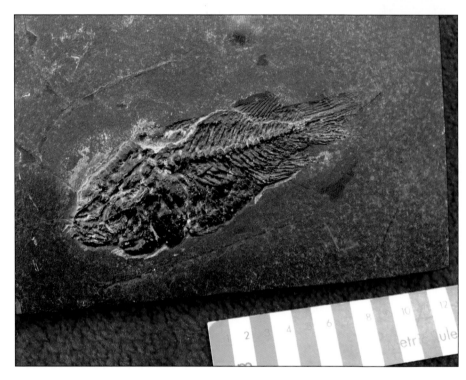

Diplomystus in oil shale from a test pit of the Green River Formation. (Value range E).

Knightia sp. Large numbers of fossil fish **impressions** like this were collected near Farson, Wyoming, from the Green River Formation from the early 1950s through the 1970s. All of these are impressions, unlike the occurrences at Fossil Butte where original bone is preserved. (Value range F).

Knightia sp. A specimen of this herring-like fish in lighter colored rock from the Green River Formation near Farson, Wyoming. Many of these were collected by rockhounds from the 1950s through the 1970s and are in collections now recycling through the collecting community. These are from the Lake Gosiute Member of the Green River Formation. (Value range F).

Knightia sp. Farson, Wyoming. Many of the fish from Farson are in hard, reddish colored rock—no original material is present on them.

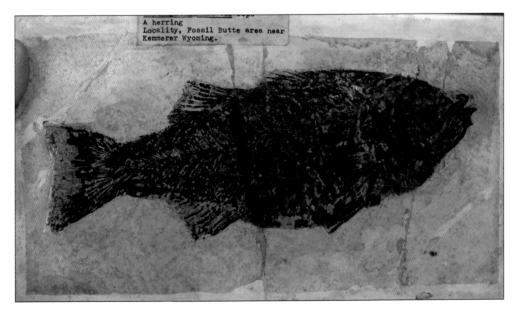

Diplomystus dentatus. A large specimen of this relatively common fish from the "fossil lake" deposits of the Green River Formation near Fossil, Wyoming. (Value range F, damaged).

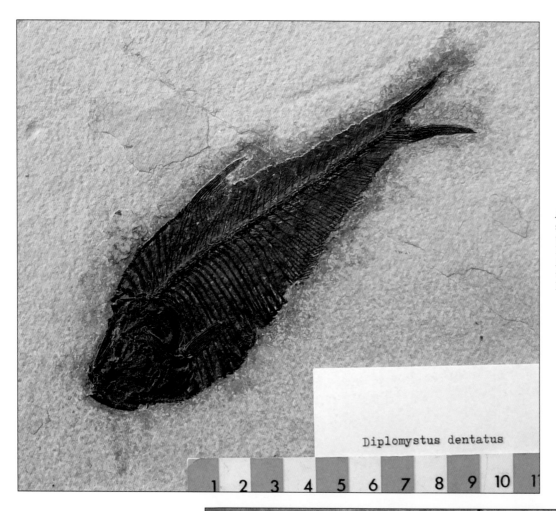

Diplomystus dentatus

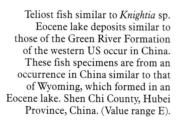

Diplomystus dentatus. Another specimen, similar to that of the previous photo from the Fossil Butte (Fossil Lake) Member, Green River Formation, Wyoming. (Value range E).

Teliost fish similar to *Knightia* sp. Eocene lake deposits similar to those of the Green River Formation of the western US occur in China. These fish specimens are from an occurrence in China similar to that of Wyoming, which formed in an Eocene lake. Shen Chi County, Hubei Province, China. (Value range E).

Florissant, Colorado, Fish

Somewhat younger in age than the Green River Formation are volcanic tuffs present near Florissant, Colorado. What are known as "park lands," rolling hills underlain by the volcanic tuffs that occur between mountains made of Precambrian granite. These "park lands," underlain by the fossil rich tuffs, are now (in part) a toney retirement and yuppie community (the comic TV series "South Park" is modeled after this area) and most of the rest of this locality has become Florissant Fossil Beds National Monument. In the lower layers of these brownish tuffs occurs a layer rich in fossil fish, predominantly bass, which lived in lakes formed by volcanic flows that dammed a waterway. The volcanic activity responsible for the flows also supplied fine ash (pyroclastic material) that preserved the fossils of Florissant.

occurrence as well as those of Lebanon and Solenhofen, Germany, originated from sediments (fine grained limestone) deposited in back reef, marine lagoons. Carbonate mud was gently deposited and the waters in these lagoons were somewhat hypersaline, a condition that was sometimes fatal to the fish. In the Monte Bolca deposits primarily tropical fish are found; however, occasional plants as well as stingrays are found, which are usually complete. The lack of high-energy water in a protected environment was one of the conditions necessary for such exceptional fossil preservation.

This fish is from the hard Eocene limestone of Monte Bolca, Italy. *Courtesy of Dept. of Earth Sciences, Washington University.*

Prisicara sp. This fish impression is from the volcanic tuffs of Florissant, Colorado. A fish fauna similar to that of the Fossil, Wyoming (Fossil Lake), deposits occur in some of the lowest fossil bearing beds of Florissant. They appear to be about the same age viz. Eocene, the same age as the Green River Formation.

Monte Bolca Fish

Evenly bedded buff, hard limestone similar to that of the Solnhofen Plattenkalk preserves fish at this Eocene locality in northern Italy. Preservation of these fish also resembles the Lower Cretaceous fossils of Lebanon, although the Monte Bolca fish are tropical fish, often full bodied forms, especially angelfish. The Monte Bolca

Another Monte Bolca fossil fish. (Value range D).

Pycnodus platessus Agassiz. Eocene, Monte Bolca, Italy.

Grube Messel Fish, Germany

North of Munich a series of Eocene lakes (formed in a graben) accumulated a thick mass of organic muck under the warm, tropical conditions of the Eocene Epoch. This organic material became a cross between brown coal and oil shale, which in the late nineteenth century was mined and retorted for petroleum, producing kerosene. During the 1920s, petroleum produced from the Messel deposits became a source for gasoline to power Germany's expanding internal-combustion-engine-based transportation. During WWII, it supplied a major portion of the petroleum for the Third Reich and mining of the deposits continued on a large scale after the war. Grube Messel lignite-oil shale accumulated in stagnant lakes around which a rich ecosystem occurred, which included mammals like small horses, bats, various marsupials, and even primitive primates. From time to time remains of these mammals fell into the lake and were buried and preserved in the organic muck, which would become the Grube Messel deposits. Over the decades, as the oil shale deposits were mined, these fossil mammals were collected and described by various paleontological workers. Much more commonly found than mammals or reptiles in the deposits are fossil fish of various types. These fossil fish come onto the collector's market from time to time where the fossil is backed up with a yellowish polyester plastic—the oil shale in which the fossils are preserved crumbling when the shale loses water and shrinks. The Grube Messel mines about twenty years ago were proposed as a landfill site; however, German fossil enthusiasts (of which there are many) fought successfully against this proposal and the area is now a fossil preserve—a preserve worked for its fossils by German museums and collectors.

Bibliography

Grande, Lance. 1984. *Paleontology of the Green River Formation, with a review of the fish fauna.* Bulletin 63. Geological Survey of Wyoming.

Hoffmann, Hillel. 2000. "Rise of Life on Earth, Messel; Window on an ancient World." *National Geographic*, Feb. 2000, pg. 34-51.

Tang, Carol M. 2002. "Monte Bolca: An Eocene Fishbowl" *in* Bottjer, Etter, Hagadorn and Tang, eds. **Exceptional Fossil Preservation**. New York: Columbia University Press.

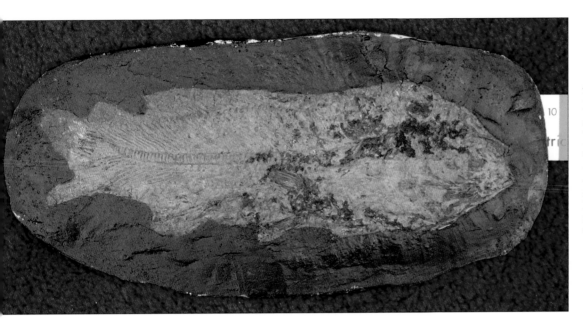

Amia kehreri (Knochen-hacht). A bowfin or fresh-water dogfish. These fish are able to tolerate stagnant water by gulping air when the oxygen level of a lake becomes low. They indicate the fetid and stagnant water conditions existing in the Grube Messel lake. Bowfins are one of the most common Grube Messel fossils. (Value range D).

Amia kehreri.
Another specimen
of this bowfin.
(Value range E).

Thaumaturus intermedius (Weitzel). Specimen showing the polyester resin in which the fossil fish are encased. This is one of the most common small fish from Grube Messel. (Value range F).

Thaumaturus intermedius (Weitzel). (Value range E).

Another specimen of the same fish as previously shown. (Value range E).

Atractosteus strausi. Gars are some of the more common fossil fish in the Grube Messel oil shale. Like bowfins, gars can tolerate stagnant, low oxygen containing water. (Value range D).

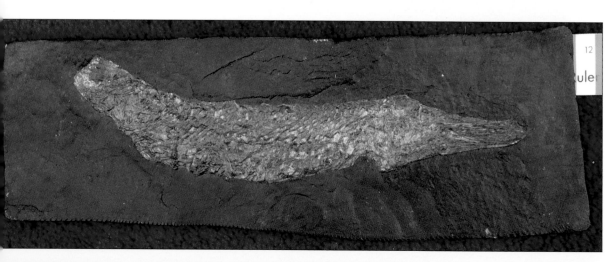

Atractosteus strausi. Another specimen of a Messel Gar pike. (Value range F).

Chapter Six

Reptiles and Birds

Turtles and Tortoises

Turtles of the Paleogene were similar in some ways to those of the late Mesozoic—the Mesozoic extinction event had not adversely affected all turtle populations. Tortoises, which are land living, heavily built turtles, became abundant during the Oligocene and later where their heavily built shells (or at least their shell fragments) can be common fossils in non-marine (terrestrial) deposits. In the Paleocene and Eocene water turtles ranged as far north as northern Canada and Alaska. In the Oligocene, large land turtles (tortoises) ranged as far as Saskatchewan. Today, large tortoises are limited to islands like the Galapagos of the eastern Pacific—all at low latitudes. The high latitude occurrences of these large turtles imply a tropical, or at least a sub-tropical, climate, whereas tortoises are limited in today's regions of cold temperatures by their inability to burrow into the ground and hibernate with the onset of winter. Large tortoises would find it impossible to burrow in this manner. Their presence, combined with plant fossils such as palms, figs, and other tropical plants, imply that the first half of the Cenozoic Era, the Paleogene, was a world where the climate was overall, even at high latitudes, warm and equitable.

Trionyx sp. A fresh water turtle of a genus that is quite common both in the early Cenozoic as well as today in rivers and lakes. Wind River Group, Upper Eocene, Moneta, Wyoming. (Value range E).

Turtle bearing sediments of the Eocene Wind River Group exposed in test pits dug for uranium exploration. Fragments of the fresh water turtle *Trionyx* were locally abundant in the bedded layers below the massive upper conglomerate (gravel) layer (top of photo). The uppermost white sample bag (for uranium content assay) lies just below the turtle-bearing layer. Poison Spider area, Rattlesnake Range, Natrona County, Wyoming, 1971.

Freshwater Eocene beds of the Wind River Group exposed in uranium exploration pits of the Rattlesnake Range, Natrona County, Wyoming, 1971.

Stylemys nebrascensis. A group of three different sized individuals of this tortoise. Brule Formation, Sioux County, Nebraska.

Stylemys nebrascensis sp. Tortoise. Tortoises of the genus *Stylemys* are the most common fossils found in the Oligocene White River Group of western Nebraska, South Dakota and eastern Wyoming. Some of these tortoises can be fairly large. (Value range F).

A small dry land Tortoise. *Testudo* sp. Leidy. Tortoises like this one, similar in size to those of today, occur in the White River Group. Also occurring are ones considerably larger than any found in the same area today. White River Group, Brule Formation. Oligocene, western Nebraska. (Value range E).

Stylemys sp. White River Group near Alcova, Natrona County, Wyoming.

Crocodilians

Crocodiles of the Cenozoic (generally) are similar to those living today, although their range was much more widespread than it is today. Crocodile fossils are found in Eocene rocks of North America as far north as northern Canada and in Alaska. This is because the climate of the Paleogene was so much warmer than it was in later geologic time or at the present. With Alaskan occurrences however, it may also be a consequence of the fact that the rocks in which they are found have moved northward to a higher latitude since they were deposited. Cenozoic strata of Alaska are generally folded and involved in tectonism—such tectonic deformation (in part) appears to be from their having moved through plate tectonics from some other part of the globe.

Crocodile—Bottom and top of a skull from Moroccan phosphate deposits. This is (probably) either Paleocene or Eocene in age, but could be as old as Cretaceous. Superb crocodile fossils occur in the Moroccan phosphate deposits, which are extensively mined near the town of Khouribga. The phosphate rich rock ranges in age from Cretaceous to Eocene—crocodiles (apparently) are found in much of this strata. As crocodiles survived the K/T extinction event, the ones found in the sandy looking phosphate rock are difficult to pin down as to age as well as to the crocodile genus. Crocodiles apparently had their greatest range during the Eocene Epoch when tropical conditions prevailed over a large portion of the globe. Oued zem, Khouribga phosphate mines, Morocco. (Value range B).

Chelonienovum ferrerei Kuntz. What appear to be the fossilized eggs of turtles or crocodiles are found preserved in calcareous mudstone of the Bouxwiller syncline "Nord de L'Alsace France." A large number of these fossil eggs have been found in Eocene mudstones; some paleontologists suggesting that they may be the eggs of turtles or snakes. They lack the calcareous shell characteristic of bird's eggs— also they are elongate like the eggs of turtles, crocodiles and snakes. (Value range E).

Crocodilus clavis Cope. A complete, large crocodile from the Eocene Bridger Formation of southwestern Wyoming. *Courtesy of Dept. of Earth and Planetary Sciences, Washington University, St. Louis.*

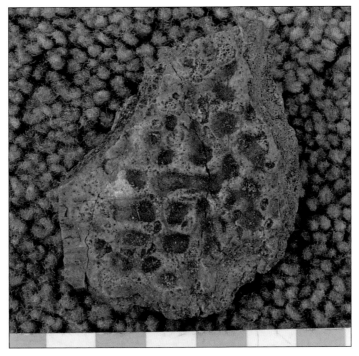

Crocodile scute. Bridger Formation, western Wyoming. Crocodile scutes like this are sporadically found in Paleogene non-marine sediments in many places—especially in those of the Eocene Epoch as the widespread warm climates at that time allowed for crocodiles to range over a large part of the earth. Similar fragmental crocodile fossils (scutes) are found in Canada and as far north as Alaska and northern Europe. (Value range G).

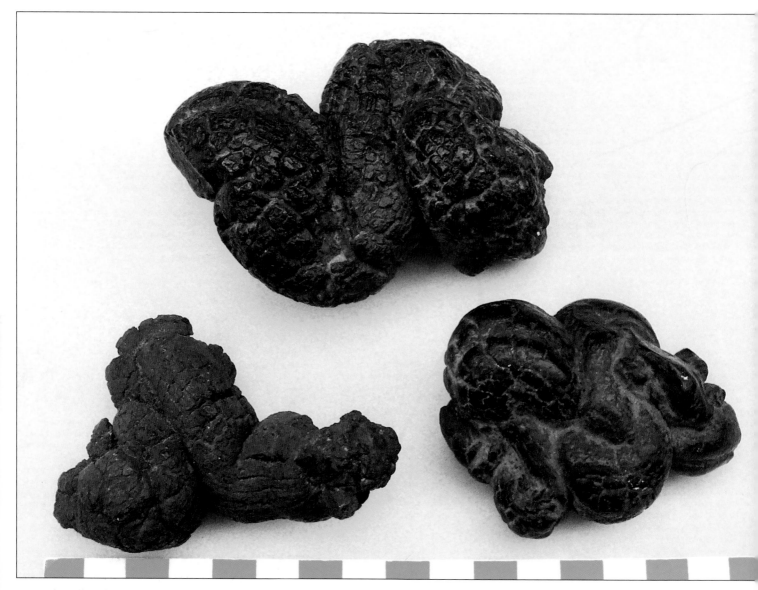

Coprolites. Oregon. These mineralized presumed reptilian turds come from a concentration of them in Oligocene strata of Oregon. They really do look "poop-like," where they are replaced with (brown) limonite. They weather out of calcareous mudstones exposed in a creek. They are also found in Miocene strata of Washington State in a similar environment. Similar examples have also recently come from Madagascar. It has recently been hypothesized that these are from manatees (sea cows) and not reptiles. (Value range G, single specimen).

Birds

Birds of many kinds were present during the early Cenozoic, however they are some of the rarest of fossils. More commonly seen are bird tracks and trackways, especially shore birds like these that walked along the fossil lakes of the Green River Formation.

Bibliography

Case, Gerard R. 1982. *A Pictorial Guide to Fossils*. New York: Van Nostrand Reinhold Company.

Hoffmann, Hillel. 2000. "Rise of Life on Earth, Messel: Window on an Ancient World." *National Geographic Magazine*, Feb. 2000, pg. 34-51.

Bird. Grube Messel. A fragmentary bird fossil from the oil shale of Grube Messel. Birds, even fragmentary ones like this, are rare fossils. Eocene lignitic oil shale of Grube Messel. (Value range E).

Another view of Grube Messel bird.

Single track rack of a large shore bird. Solders Summit, Utah. Large numbers of these trackways occur on slabs of silty limestone formed from extensive limy "mudflats" of the Lake Unita portion of the Green River Formation. Large numbers of shore birds walked on these mudflats, leaving these tracks and trackways. Today these mudflat beds are exposed in a series of road and stream outcrops near Solders Summit, Utah. (Value range F).

Shorebird trackway. Solders Summit, Utah, Green River Formation. (Value range E)

Shorebird trackway, Green River Formation, Solders Summit, Utah.

Chapter Seven

Mammals

Dawn Horse

Shown here is a portion of the jaw of a small (one foot high) Eocene horse.

Hyracotherium sp. A jaw fragment of the dawn horse. Eocene, Wind River Group, Lysite Member, Natrona County, Wyoming.

White River Group Badlands

One of the largest and best known Paleogene mammal faunas in the world occurs in the White River Group of the high plains of western Nebraska, eastern Wyoming, South Dakota, and southern Saskatchewan. The White River Group represents a series of stream deposited mudstones and sandstone deposited by eastward flowing streams carrying sediment derived from the uplift of parts of the Rocky Mountains. These freshwater, fluvial deposits can locally be eroded into a series of large gullies known as badlands that occur adjacent to streams, which have eroded into them. The White River Group carries one of the largest and best-known late Eocene and Oligocene mammal faunas in the world and its strata extends over a large area. Outcrops of the white mudstones of the Group can be relatively abundant in the arid terrain of the high plains. The White River Group consists of two major units (formations), the older Chadron Formation and the overlying Brule Formation. The White River Group has conventionally been considered as Oligocene in age; however, many workers now consider the Chadron as Upper Eocene in age. The reason for this change is that the Chardon contains Brontotheres (also known as titanotheres) and these large mammals appear diagnostic of the Eocene Epoch, going extinct at its end.

The best known area of outcrop of the White River Group is the Big Badlands (*Mauvases Terres*) of South Dakota. This area, much of which is in the Big Badlands National Monument, is closed to fossil collecting. Badland areas of both the Chadron and Brule Formations also occur on private land, as well as the Pine Ridge and Rosebud Indian Reservations. Some of the private lands in this area are open to collecting, for a fee.

Typical outcrop of mudstone of the White River Group eroded into badlands, central South Dakota.

White River Group Mammals Related to Living Forms

These are mammal fossils (generally small) which are related to living mammals such as the deer, horse, and camel. Even though the Cenozoic is known as the age of mammals, fossil mammals generally are less common in its strata than are those of reptiles (specifically turtles) and these are much less common than are invertebrates—the most commonly seen Cenozoic fossils.

Palaeolagus sp. "Paleobunny." (Value range G).

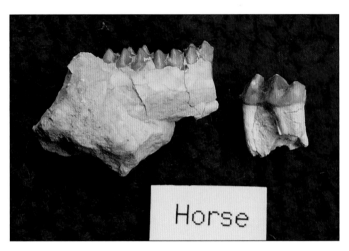

Mesohippus sp. Horse. Brule Formation, White River Group. This represents a different species of "dawn horse," younger than the previously illustrated jaw fragment. (Value range F).

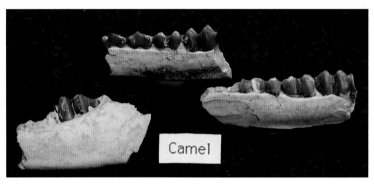

Stenomylus gracilis, camel. The camel, as well as the horse, makes its earliest appearance in North America. (Value range G, single jaw fragment).

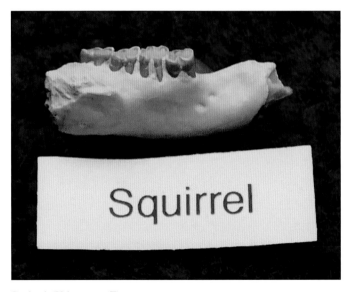

Squirrel. (Value range F).

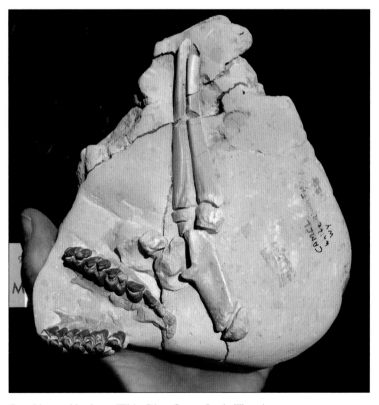

Camel jaw and leg bone. White River Group, Lusk, Wyoming. (Value range E).

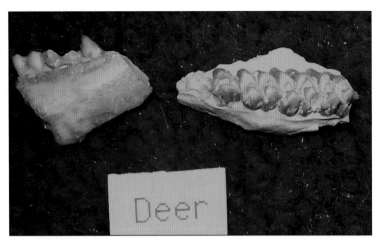

"Paleo-Deer."

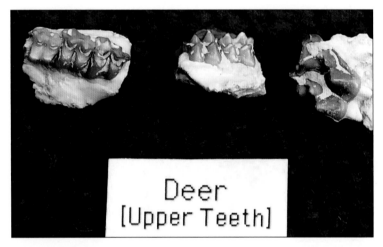

Deer (upper teeth).

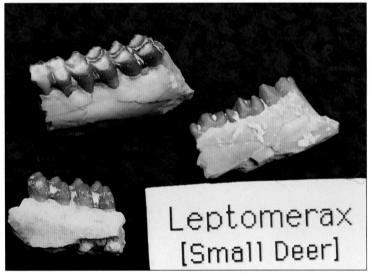

Leptomeryx sp. (Small "deer.")

Oreodonts

The most common fossil mammals in the Brule Formation are oreodonts, an extinct family of mammals. Oreodonts represent one of a number of mammal types (families) that fell to extinction at the end of the Paleogene to a major extinction event.

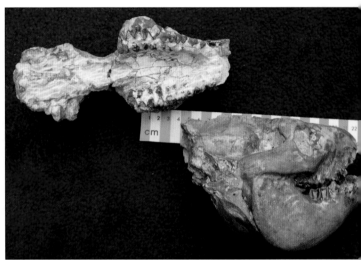

Merycoidodon culbertsonii. Typical skulls of this widespread fossil of the Brule Formation. The oreodont is probably the most commonly seen Oligocene mammal of the White River Group, Lusk, Wyoming.

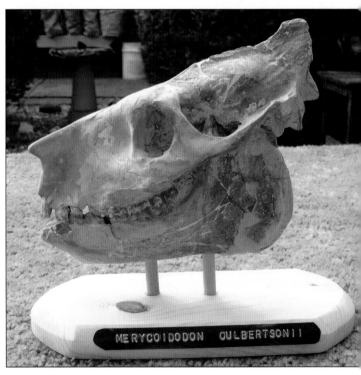

Merycoidodon culbertsonii. Oreodont, Oligocene, White River Group, Brule Formation, South Dakota. (Value range D).

Merycoidodon culbert-sonii. Large fragment-ed skull from a large individual, which is partially prepared. Central South Dakota. (Value range F).

Partially repaired skull of *Merycoidodon* sp. Lusk, Wyoming. (Value range F).

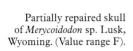

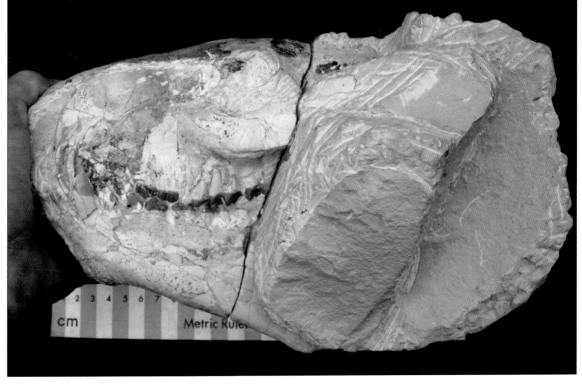

Group of partial oreodont skulls. The condition of the majority of oreodont skulls found in the Brule Formation, Crawford, Nebraska.

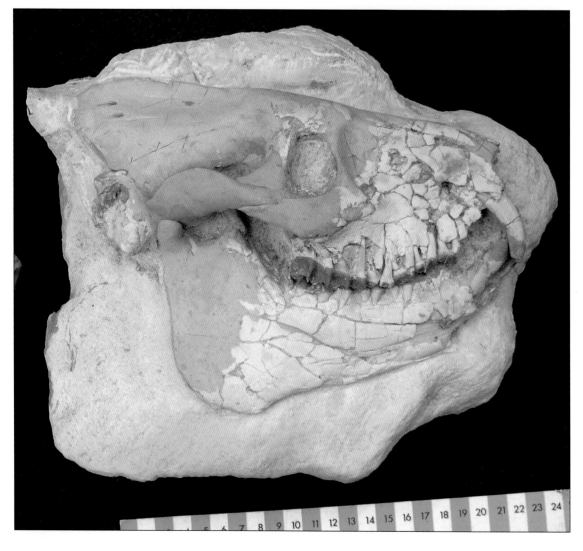

Merycoidodon skull in a nodule-like mass. (Specimen repaired and reconstructed). (Value range F).

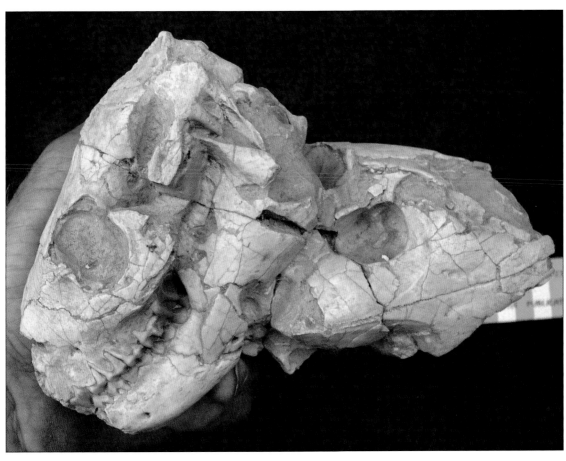

Two skulls of *Merycoidodon culbertsonii* pressed together. Oreodonts are found grouped together or clustered together in some occurrences. Brule Formation, Lusk, Wyoming. (Value range E).

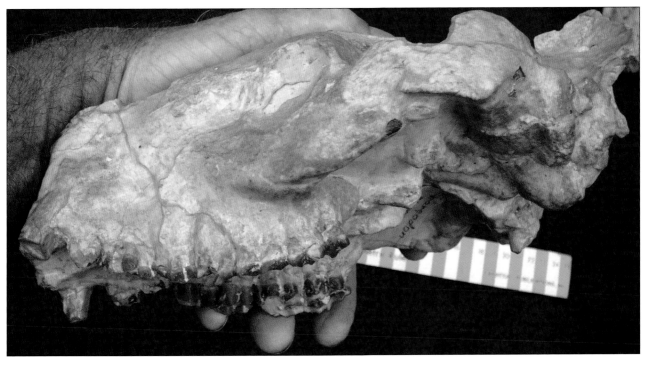

Merycoidodon sp. A large species of this common oreodont species. (Value range E).

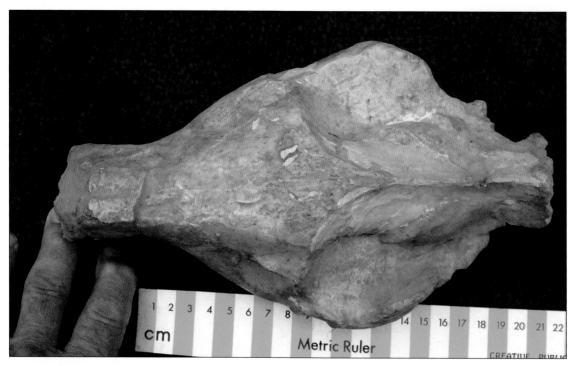

Top view of skull in the previous photo.

Presented here is a scatter of oreodont skulls from the Brule Formation,
from various localities in the White River Group.

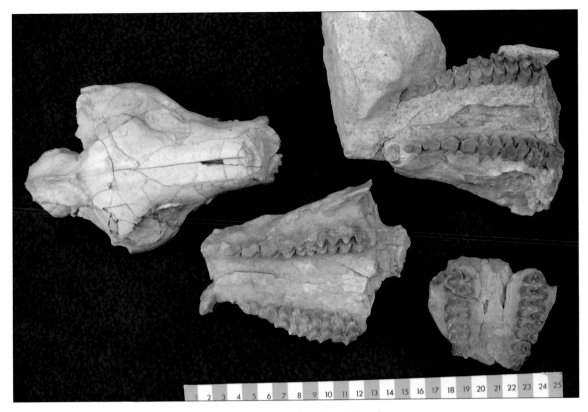

Right: upper palettes of oreodont skulls; left: top of incomplete skull. Lusk, Wyoming.

Merycoidodon sp. Natural brain cast. White River Group, central South Dakota. (Value range F).

Oreodont—lower jaw. Crawford, Nebraska. (Value range E).

Pigs

Oreodonts have been stated as being a type of pig, which they are not! Here is the skull of an actual Paleogene pig from the Chadron Formation of the White River Group.

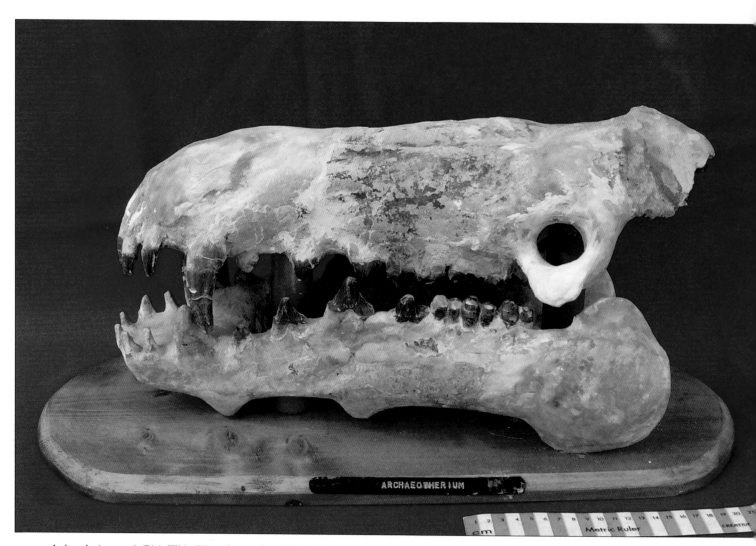

Archaeotherium scotti. (Pig). White River Group, Central South Dakota. (Value range D).

Titanotheres

Titanotheres, like oreodonts, represent an extinct mammal group of the early Cenozoic. Titanotheres were one of the largest of Paleogene mammals.

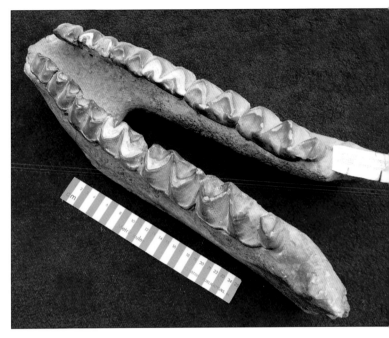

Titanothere jaw—same specimen as in left photo with different lighting.

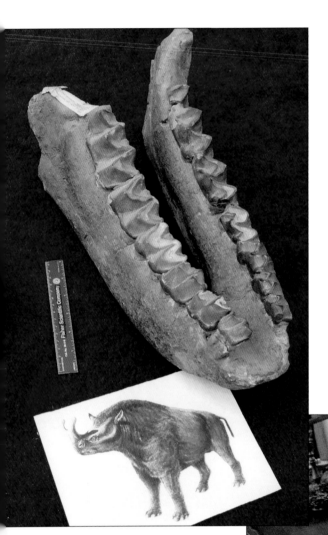

Titanothere lower jaw, Chadron Formation. Titanothere skulls and jaws are one of the more desirable mammal fossils from White River Group strata. This is from an outlier of it near Alcova, Wyoming, which would now be considered as late Eocene in age as titanotheres are now believed to have went extinct at the end of the Eocene Epoch. (Value range D).

Brontotherium (*Brontops*) sp. (Titanothere skull). Upper Eocene, White River Group, Chadron Formation. The Chadron Formation has conventionally been considered as Oligocene in age. The brontotheres are now considered (by vertebrate paleontologists) to be strictly an Eocene mammal, so that would make the Chadron Formation latest Eocene rather than Oligocene in age. Western South Dakota. (Value range C).

Titanothere leg bones. This group of titanothere leg bones came from a concentration of them near Alcova, Wyoming. This assemblage is mounted as it occurred in an outlier of the Chadron Formation. (Value range E).

Titanothere leg, Chadron Formation outlier near Alcova, Wyoming. (Value range E).

Brontops sp. Titanothere foot bones, South Dakota. *Courtesy of Dept. of Earth and Planetary Sciences, Washington University, St. Louis.*

Rhinoceros

True rhinoceroses are found in the Paleogene. Fossil bones of them can be locally common fossils in sediments of the White River Group. Complete rhinoceros skulls, like most other White River fossil skulls, are quite desirable.

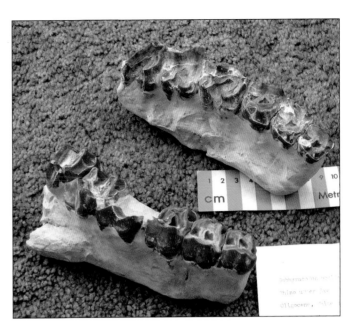

Subhyracodon occidentalis. Rhinoceros—upper jaw. White River Group, South Dakota. (Value range E).

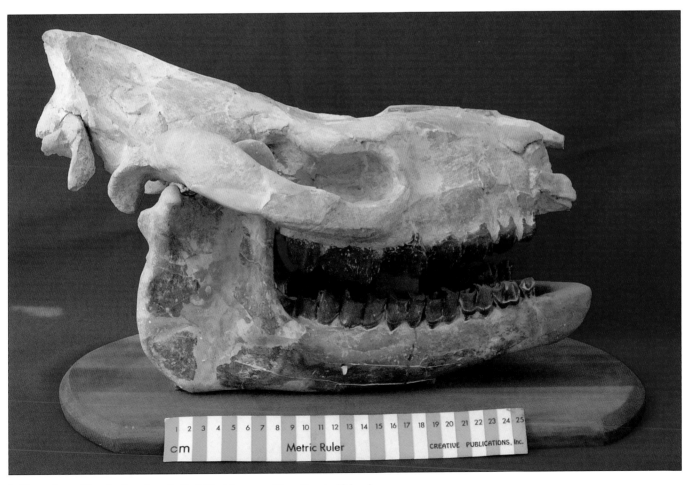

Subhyracodon occidentalis. Complete skull of this rhinoceros. Sioux County, Nebraska. (Value range C).

156

Saber Tooth Tiger

Fossils of predatory mammals generally are rare fossils. Herbivores, being numerically more abundant than predators, are more likely to leave a fossil record. Also predators, being more intelligent, are generally less prone to being killed by events such as floods or other fossil-making events, which might kill a less intelligent herbivore. Oligocene saber tooth cats are only distantly related to the true saber tooth cats of the Pleistocene Epoch. These earlier cats are often referred to as "false" saber tooth cats.

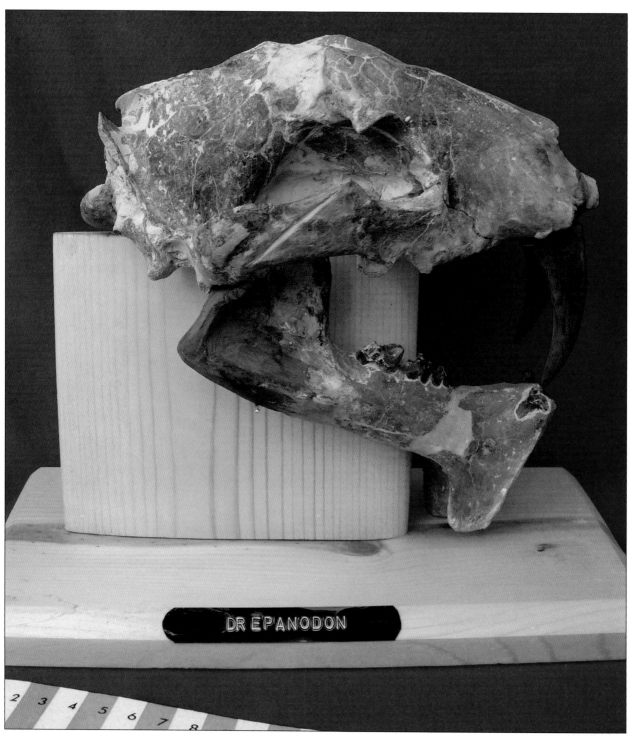

Drepanodon sp. Fake saber tooth tiger. Skulls of these cats are one of the most desirable fossils from the White River Group. White River Group, Brule Formation.

Grube Messel Mammals

A lignitic oil shale series in Germany was mined for many years as a source of petroleum. As a consequence of this activity, a number of significant early Cenozoic mammal fossils have come to light. The Grube Messel locality of late Eocene age has been one of the most extensive sources for early mammals. Grube Messel fossils are usually backed or set in a slab of polyester resin as, once the oil shale in which they are found dries out, the shale becomes very crumbly.

Bibliography

Benton, Michael. 1991. *The Rise of the Mammals*. London: Quantum Publishing Ltd.

Boyce, Japheth B. *Japh's Pretty Good Fossil Book of the Dakota Territory*. Rapid City, South Dakota: RJB Rock Shop.

Case, Gerald. C. 1988. *A Pictorial Guide to Fossils*. New York, New York: Van Nostrand Rheinhold Co.

Hay, Oliver Perry. 1908. *The Fossil Turtles of North America*. Washington, D.C.: Carnegie Institution of Washington. (Reprint, 2006 The Center for North American Herpetology.)

O'Harra, Clleophas C. 1920. "The White River Badlands." *South Dakota School of Mines, Bulletin No. 13*. Versions (reprints) of this work are still available at various locations in South Dakota.

Scott, James. 1978. *Paleontology*. New York, New York: Taplinger Publishing Co.

Microparamys parvus. Grube Messel, Germany (**cast**). An early rodent from this oil shale-lignite deposit. Many mammals, being active, intelligent animals, often avoid those pitfalls that would otherwise allow them to be killed and buried to become a fossil. This well made cast would be difficult to distinguish from the real thing. Articulated mammals such as this are rare fossils and some of the most complete ones have come from the oil shale of Grube Messel, Germany. (A complete specimen of an early primate from Messel recently (2009) was given a lot of attention in the media). (Value range E, as cast).

Bat. Messel, Germany. Bats generally are rare fossils. This is a partial bat skeleton from the Grube Messel oil shale. Early Cenozoic bats appear to have been similar to those living today. Bats, of course, represent an adaptation for flight independent of that of birds and pterodactyls. (Value range E, rare).

Glossary

Atlantic coastal plain sediments: A series of sediments (generally soft and poorly indurated) that were deposited when the Atlantic Ocean covered parts of eastern North America. Atlantic coastal plain sediments are similar to those of the Gulf Series and contain similar fossils, sometimes in abundance.

Badlands: A maze of gullies, spires, and other erosional phenomena carved by running water in beds of clay, mudstone, and soft sandstone, usually of terrestrial origin. Badlands are particularly characteristic of arid regions and can be a prolific source of fossil vertebrates as well as plants of Cenozoic age. One of the largest Cenozoic badlands is the *Mauvases Terres* or Big Badlands of South Dakota. Badlands of Cenozoic age are also known in Africa, associated with the Sahara Desert. They are also found in China, Mongolia, and South America (Patagonia).

Bryophytes: A major category of plants (Division) consisting of small ground dwelling forms that reproduce by spores and fruiting bodies. Bryophytes appear to be primitive plants and are generally considered to be the mosses. The liverworts (*hepatophytes*) are sometimes included with the bryophytes by some, particularly more conservative taxonomists. Both mosses and liverworts are believed to have existed on the earth's surface earlier than did more complex plants like ferns and lycopods; however, the fossil record of bryophytes and liverworts is extremely sparse.

Burnout: Clay or shale which overlies a coal or lignite seam that has been baked or fired by spontaneous combustion of the underlying coal. Shale or clay beds that overlie coal beds (seams) can sometimes contain well-preserved fossil leaves. These can occur in burnout as leaf impressions in a brick red rock. Burnout (also known as clinker) commonly occurs in the Paleocene Fort Union Group of the northern North American High Plains.

Concretion: A hard, calcareous (limestone-like) elliptical shaped rock that often forms around a nucleus, which can be a fossil. With regard to marine Cenozoic fossils and strata, the nucleus-forming fossil sometimes can be a crab or a lobster. Fossil crustaceans in Cenozoic strata are often found forming a concretions nucleus.

Compression fossil: A fossil (usually leaves of plants) in which the leaf (or fish, etc.) is flattened (compressed) on a layer of rock (bedding plane) with some of the original material of the organism being preserved as a carbon or carbonaceous film or residue. A compression fossil is in contrast to an impression fossil, where no original organic material is preserved.

Correlatives: (as in correlation of strata). The process (often using fossils) of tying strata of different regions together in terms of their being of the same geologic age. Strata correlation attempts to determine that rock strata of two different regions or of different types were actually deposited during the same span of geologic time.

Epoch: A subdivision of geologic time of lower rank than a geologic period like the Cretaceous (and also shorter in geologic time). Epochs are especially utilized in the Cenozoic Era to delineate its subdivisions. The earliest half of the Cenozoic Era, the Paleogene, is composed of the Paleocene, Eocene, and the Oligocene Epochs.

Foraminifera: A class of single celled protists which posses a calcareous "shell" or "test." Fossil foraminifera are utilized to index marine strata, especially in the petroleum industry as their tiny shells can survive the drilling process, where they are used to determine the geologic age of strata being drilled during petroleum exploration. Some foraminifera (forams) of the Cenozoic can be especially large—usually, however, foraminifera are microfossils.

Genus: A category in biological classification (taxonomy) above the **species** level and the higher rank of a two part (binomial) biological name.

Graben: A portion of the Earth's crust that has moved downward, often as a consequence of being in tension. A graben will be bounded by faults, the side of the fault facing the graben being known as the down dropped side. Grabens can accumulate sediment, which may be the sediments of a lake bottom. Such an environment can preserve exceptional fossils, the Eocene deposits of Grube Messel of Germany being deposited in such a setting.

Greywacke: Sandy sediment often referred to as dirty sandstone—clay, mud or volcanic ash may occur as impurities along with quartz sand. For our discussion, this is used in reference to Eocene plant bearing strata of Alaska, where coal bearing beds of greywacke have been preserved from erosion in down dropped blocks of the Earth's crust.

Group and Formation: In reference to strata, a **formation** is a sequence of sedimentary rock that has some sort of "common denominator," which can be mapped and represented on a geologic map. A **group** is a collection of formations that are all within a restricted portion of geologic time. Rock strata of the Earth's crust are named and classified in a manner similar to that used in classifying organisms in biology. The formation is the fundamental unit of classification much as the species is in the biological Linnean system.

Gulf Series: A sequence of late Mesozoic strata that continues into the Cenozoic Era and includes both the early (Paleogene) and late Cenozoic (Neogene). Sediments of the Gulf Series make up the coastal plain surrounding the Gulf of Mexico. Gulf Series sediments can sometimes be richly fossiliferous, but often they are not well exposed because of vegetal cover and their softness. They can be quite thick surrounding the Gulf of Mexico and are a prolific source of petroleum, much of which is produced offshore.

Herbaceous Angiosperms: Seed bearing plants (angiosperms) that are smaller than trees, generally growing near ground level. Small seed bearing plants are rare in the early Cenozoic; its plant fossil record is almost entirely made up of tree-sized plants. There is a question as to just how extensive seed bearing ground plants were during the early Cenozoic—ground vegetation at that time seems to still have been primarily ferns.

Hypersaline environment or conditions: An environment under which sediment is deposited where a greater than normal amount of salt (salinity) is present. Specifically, in the early Cenozoic's Green River Formation of Wyoming and Utah, the lake, which covered large parts of these states (Lake Uinta), was hypersaline and had a salinity that often exceeded that of seawater. Under these **hypersaline conditions,** few organisms could live. One that did was the cyanobacteria (blue green algae), which formed stromatolites, now preserved as fossils.

Indurated vs. non-indurated sediment: Having to do with how hard or cemented a sedimentary rock is, indurated sedimentary rocks are hard! Those of the Cenozoic Era are often soft or poorly indurated—especially those Cenozoic rocks that have not been involved with tectonic activity. Tectonic activity, such as folding, faulting, and deep burial, will usually make a sedimentary rock much harder. Cenozoic sedimentary rocks are otherwise generally soft and poorly indurated.

K/T extinction event: The end of the Mesozoic Era (67 million years ago) is marked by extinction of many dominant life forms, which included ammonites, rudistids, dinosaurs, and pterodactyls—to name a few. This extinction, one of the major extinctions in the history of life, has been variously attributed to volcanic activity, ecological collapse, and more recently to an asteroid impact that set off a series of ecological disasters. The K in K/T refers to the Cretaceous Period (on geological maps Cretaceous rocks are indicated by a K to prevent confusion with those of the Carboniferous, which are indicated by a C). The T stands for the Tertiary Period of the Cenozoic Era. The Tertiary is made up of the Paleocene, Eocene, Oligocene, Miocene, and Pliocene Epochs. The K/T extinction event marks the beginning of the Cenozoic Era.

Lignite: Often referred to as "brown coal," lignite is a coal-like rock that is somewhat intermediate between coal and the original plant debris, the source of coal. Lignite is especially characteristic of the Cenozoic Era, where in many parts of the globe it is mined as a fossil fuel.

Outlier: A remnant of younger strata that otherwise would have been eroded away. In terms of this work, it refers to isolated remnants of bone bearing Oligocene (or late Eocene) strata found in Wyoming and South Dakota. Such remnants of younger strata are often preserved by being part of a downward moving block of the Earth's crust known as a graben. Outliers can also occur at the topographically highest part of a region such as at the top of a butte.

Resins, fossil: A general term for terpenoid or succinate resins derived from either coniferous trees or from resin producing angiosperms. Included under this term are amber, succinite, and copalite. Coniferous derived resins occur in quantity in lignite and/or coal of Paleocene age of the Fort Union Group and its correlatives. These fossil resins are the feedstock from which is derived cresylic acid used in making plastics.

Solenhofen Plattenkalk: A series of late Jurassic slabby limestone, which preserved marine fossils with exceptional fidelity, deposited in a back reef lagoon. Other, similar occurrences with exceptional fossils are the Cretaceous beds of Lebanon and slabby Eocene strata of Monte Bolca of northern Italy.

Stratigraphy: The art and science of recognition and classification of rock strata of the Earth's crust. Stratigraphy uses a hierarchical system similar to that of the Linnean system of organismic classification of biology. In stratigraphy the formation is the fundamental unit of classification: Lower Taxonomic levels include the member, layer, and zone; higher taxonomic levels are the Group and Series; and then finally the major subdivisions of geologic time itself, the Period and the Era.

Stromatolite: A structure (trace fossil) produced by the physiological activity of cyanobacteria (blue green algae). Stromatolites represent the oldest direct evidence of life, some being found in strata as ancient as 3.5 billion years. In the Cenozoic Era extensive stromatolite "reefs" occur in the Green River Formation where they formed in large lakes. Similar Paleogene lake deposits with stromatolites occur in strata in other parts of the world as well; stromatolites however are generally rare in Cenozoic limestone.

Terrestrial or Terriginous Sediment: Sediment (or sedimentary rock) made of clay, silt or sand deposited in a fresh water environment on a continent or other large land mass. In contrast to marine sediment, which in the Cenozoic was usually deposited at the edge of a landmass when its margins were below sea level and were covered by shallow seas, terrestrial sediments of Cenozoic age may carry fossils of land animals, especially those of mammals, turtles, and plants. In arid regions, such terriginous sediment may be eroded into a series of gullies, ravines, and spires known as "badlands."

Workers: A term used in paleontology to refer to paleontologists who work on a specific group of organisms. For instance, a person might be a "worker" on dinosaurs or on sponges. The term specialist—as used in the medical profession—is applicable here. A worker is a paleontological specialist.

Oligocene landscape, Wyoming. *Artwork by Elizabeth Stinchcomb.*